RENÉE T. FRANTZEN
RAGGEDY ANN
A PERPETUAL QUEST, VOLUME 1

Copyright © 2025 by Renée T. Frantzen.

All rights reserved. No part of this book may be reproduced in any form or by any electronic or mechanical means, including information storage and retrieval systems, without permission in writing from the publisher, except by reviewers, who may quote brief passages in a review.

This publication contains the opinions and ideas of its author. It is intended to provide helpful and informative material on the subjects addressed in the publication. The author and publisher specifically disclaim all responsibility for any liability, loss, or risk, personal or otherwise, which is incurred as a consequence, directly or indirectly, of the use and application of any of the contents of this book.

MILTON & HUGO L.L.C.
4407 Park Ave., Suite 5
Union City, NJ 07087, USA

Website: www. miltonandhugo.com
Hotline: 1- 888-778-0033
Email: info@miltonandhugo.com

Ordering Information:
Quantity sales. Special discounts are available on quantity purchases by corporations, associations, and others. For details, contact the publisher at the address above.

Library of Congress Control Number: 2025909233
ISBN-13:   979-8-89285-309-5   [Paperback Edition]
            979-8-89285-552-5   [Paperback Edition]
            979-8-89285-308-8   [Digital Edition]

Rev. date: 05/12/2025

RAGGEDY ANN

A PERPETUAL QUEST, VOLUME 1

RENÉE T. FRANTZEN

ABOUT THE AUTHOR
Renée T. Frantzen

Serious collecting of Raggedy Ann and Andy memorabilia did not start until 1985; the year I graduated college and met my husband, Brian. However, I received my first Raggedy Ann doll, a Knickerbocker, for Christmas in 1971, four days shy of my sixth birthday. For Christmas 1972 two Andies came to our house. One was for me and the other one was for my older brother. My brother was not interested in his Andy so I inherited him and I still have both along with my first Raggedy Ann. People have asked "why Raggedy Ann and Andy?", and I don't have an answer. They just appeal to me.

In 1989 I attended a doll show and purchased Susan Garrison's book **The Raggedy Ann and Andy Family Album**. After reading her book and noticing the picture captions "from the collection of…" I knew there were more people interested in Raggedy Ann and Andy because the pictures were of items I had never seen. I went to the library to do research on Raggedy Ann (this is before the worldwide web) but only found one article in **Doll Reader** magazine, which stated there was a RAGS newsletter. This newsletter was started in 1988 by a woman in Georgia named Barbara Barth. I was able to contact her and she set me up with a subscription. I also obtained back issues from which I learned about an annual Raggedy Ann and Andy Festival held in Arcola, Illinois, the first one taking place in 1987.

Arcola is the birthplace of Johnny Gruelle (born December 24, 1880), the author and illustrator of the first Raggedy Ann book. (Johnny was also a Christmas baby, maybe that is where the connection started). The Raggedy Ann and Andy Museum was also in Arcola. That was founded by Joni Gruelle Wannamaker (granddaughter of Johnny Gruelle) and her husband Tom in 1999 (closed in 2009). Some of the museum's contents were donated to the Strong National Museum of Play; other parts of the collection are still in Arcola at Rockome Gardens Theme Park. Joni has a brother named Kim who had a store in the Blue Ridge Mountains of North Carolina. Kim attended several Raggedy Ann and Andy Festivals in Arcola.

Brian and I missed the first three festivals because we did not know about them. In 1991, I attended the fourth festival alone to save on airfare in case it was a dud. It wasn't. In 1992 we attended the fifth festival and every festival after that, until they stopped in 2009.

In 1996 my collection was featured in an article in our local newspaper, **Newsday**. F.A.O. Schwartz in New York City hosted Raggedy Ann's 90th birthday in September 2005. Joni Wannamaker and her aunt, Ruth Gruelle were there. Joni read a story. In 2007, The Ward Melville Heritage Organization, a cultural center in Stony Brook, New York had an exhibit featuring Raggedy Ann and Andy and ice cream. The director of that Center first contacted Joni and Tom Wannamaker asking if they would be able to offer items for display. They were not able to because of the distance. However, they gave the director my name and number and she called me. My husband and I rented a U-Haul 10' box truck and brought many pieces (not even half of my collection) to the Center. The items were on display for one month. A Saturday tea party was held for young girls. I attended dressed as Raggedy Ann and the girls were in their costumes as well. There was also a story hour, where a retired school teacher read **The Real for Sure Story of Raggedy Ann** and **The Real for Sure Story of Raggedy Andy,** both written by Patricia Hall and illustrated by Joni Gruelle. September 2010 marked the 95th birthday of Raggedy Ann. The Strong Museum of Play in Rochester, New York had a celebration, which we attended as well. On March 27, 2002, Raggedy Ann was inducted into the National Toy Hall of Fame at the Strong National Museum of Play in Rochester, NY.

Johnny Gruelle's father was from Cynthiana, Kentucky which hosted a few festivals but those have ceased as well. Raggedy gatherings have been held in Florida, Missouri, Nebraska, North Carolina, Ohio and Pennsylvania. The only social event still taking place is an annual Raggedy Rally held in Arthur, Illinois in June.

Several collectors also sport tattoos of Raggedy Ann and Andy. I am one of them. I have a tattoo of Raggedy Ann and Andy dancing on my left shoulder blade. One of my collector friends lives in Florida and her collection was featured on The Learning Channel in a show called "My Crazy Obsession". There are even collectors from Japan. Magazines with Raggedy Ann and Andy as the subject have been published in Japan and the collections of the Japanese readers have been featured.

Barbara Barth published RAGS Newsletter from her home in Georgia. After several years it was overwhelming so she passed the files to Rankin Publishing in Arcola, Illinois. Rankin published RAGS for several years and in October 2008 they passed the files to Castle Press Publications, which also publishes **Doll Castle News** magazine. Dorita Mortensen is the editor and unfortunately, Dorita and her associates decided the interest in just Raggedy Ann and Andy was not as profitable as dolls in general so publishing of RAGS ceased in 2011. No other publishers continued publishing.

My 10,000 piece collection consists of advertisements, articles, barrettes, blankets, books, bowls, boxes, buttons, cans, candles, cards, cartoons, clothing, coloring books, comic books, cookie jars, craft kits, cups, curtains, decals, dishes, display fixtures, fabric, food (unopened packages or just the packaging), furniture, games, jewelry, lamps, lunch boxes, magazines, magnets, movies, music, music boxes, ornaments, patches, patterns, pictures, pillows, planters, plaques, postcards, puzzles, rubber stamps, rugs, salt and pepper shakers, sheet sets, soap, stationery, tea sets, t-shirts, towels, toys, utensils, wallpaper, wrapping paper, and, of course, lots of dolls. The collection is catalogued and insured. I have pictures of each item in a PowerPoint presentation. The description, where purchased, when purchased, price paid and markings are in an Excel spreadsheet. When I attended the Festivals in Arcola, I carried a binder which contained the PowerPoint pictures so I could refer to them to prevent purchasing duplicates. All my Raggedy acquaintances knew what was in the binder and asked if they could look through it. They also asked if I had purchased additional items from the previous year. I shared whenever time allowed and said, of course, the Raggedys welcomed new family members.

When Brian and I moved into our apartment in Commack, New York there was a separate room which I used to display the Raggedies. Collectors say "there is always room for one more". After several years, it became difficult to walk into that room because items were being stacked in boxes in lieu of displayed. I used other rooms in the apartment but had to be resourceful in displaying items. For jewelry, I purchased a screen kit at Home Depot. For pillows and ornaments I purchased plastic chains which were hung from the ceiling with plastic clips (available where laundry care products are sold). Ephemera, although not on display, can be easily viewed as the items are in plastic sheet protectors with various-sized openings.

In 2017, Brian passed away. I continued to live in the apartment we shared with my Raggedies. I also still attend the Raggedy Rally in Arcola, Illinois every year. In 2020, I met Douglas. He has become enamored with the Raggedies and has learned to "spot" them at various markets and shows. In September 2023 Douglas had to sell the house he shared with his mother because she passed away. My father offered a place for us to live (my childhood home in Greenlawn, New York). The Raggedies were packed up and utilizing two U-Haul trucks on two Saturdays we conducted Raggedy relocations. Some of the items are on display in my father's house. From the items that are still in boxes I can hear them crying and saying, "please let us out". My dream is to have a Raggedy house someday.

If you like to travel, doll shows, garage sales and flea markets like Renniger's in Pennsylvania and Florida and Brimfield in Massachusetts are good places for Raggedies. If cyber shopping is your thing eBay and Raggedy Land (www.raggedyland.com) are good sites for researching and purchasing.

If you are a baby boomer, you certainly know who Raggedy Ann and Raggedy Andy are. They were conceived when your grandparents were adolescents and have survived the test of time for over 100 years. Other characters have joined their "family" but they are not as popular. There is something about these two redheads that keeps them in everyone's thoughts. When I am asked what drew me to collecting them, my answer is "I just like them". They were created as dolls. If they were human one could say they have genetically changed over time, i.e. hair color, skin color, height, clothing and sock patterns, and facial expressions. While there are 800+ dolls in my collection, dolls aren't the only item this sister and brother team have come to in realization. Manufacturers in industries such as bedding, kitchenware, clothing, toys, printing, home décor, crafts, furniture, jewelry, et al. have been involved in using Raggedy Ann and Raggedy Andy as either marketing tools or adornments in their products. If you would like to see the many products produced, peruse this volume. Perhaps you want to start a collection or add a redhead or two to your life. The items pictured are not for sale, nor are values shown. There are plenty of places to start your own collection and it's what you want to pay that sets the value. When I started this project, I was hoping to produce one book. That is not possible for numerous reasons. This book covers only the items in my collection that start with the letter A. I hope to produce more volumes creating a series where each subsequent book focuses on the next letter of the alphabet.

I wish to thank my parents, my late husband, Brian, who never stopped me from purchasing "another one for my collection", my boyfriend, Douglas, who has become an expert spotter in just four years and other Raggedy collectors who always said "you should write a book, your collection is so organized". Although I had pictures already of every item in my collection when I started this project, not every picture was clear. Thanks to Google, Facebook, eBay and other websites, I was able to obtain better pictures, a lot coming from pictures other collectors had posted, namely Raggedy Land, Nancy Nelson, Andrew Tabbat, Patricia Hall, Raggedys and Teddys, Ron and Sherry Rasmussen, Gordon Nichols, Raggedy John, Diane and Jed Ashton, Tony and Phyllis Nestor, Hiromi Nishizawa, Beverly Spadaro.

ITEM	SIZE
Advertisement - 10th Annual Raggedy Ann and Andy Festival	5½ x 8½

MANUFACTURER/MARKING

Arcola Chamber of Commerce, May 22-23, 1999

ITEM	SIZE
Advertisement - 10th Raggedy Ann and Andy Walk, Arcola, Illinois	5½ x 8½

MANUFACTURER/MARKING

ITEM	SIZE
Advertisement - 11th Raggedy Ann and Andy Festival, 11th Celebration Dinner, Happy 85th	8½ x 11

MANUFACTURER/MARKING

Raggedy Ann and Andy Festival 1990-2000

ITEM	SIZE
Advertisement - 12th Annual Raggedy Ann and Andy Festival Schedule of Events	5½ x 8½

MANUFACTURER/MARKING

Arcola, Illinois, May 19 and 20, 2001

ITEM	SIZE
Advertisement - 14" Camel with the Wrinkled Knees, 17" Raggedy Ann and Raggedy Andy and Little Brown Bear	8 x 11½

MANUFACTURER/MARKING
R. John Wright Dolls, Inc., Bennington, VT, Simon & Schuster, Inc., licensed by United Media

ITEM	SIZE
Advertisement - 16 inch Dolls and Raggedy Ann talking doll	8⅛ x 11

MANUFACTURER/MARKING
1974 Spiegel

ITEM	SIZE
Advertisement - 1995 Raggedy Ann and Andy Festival Brunch, yellow	8½ x 11

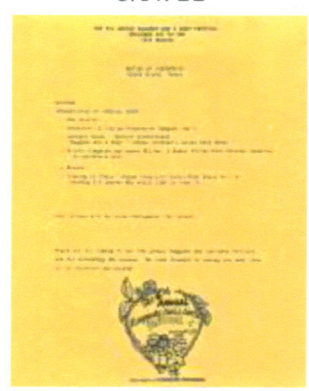

MANUFACTURER/MARKING
Schedule of Events

ITEM	SIZE
Advertisement - 1995 Raggedy Ann and Andy Festival Schedule of Events, yellow	8½ x 11

MANUFACTURER/MARKING
Schedule of Events

ITEM

Advertisement - 1996 Raggedy Ann and Andy Festival Toyland Parade Registration Form

SIZE

8½ x 11

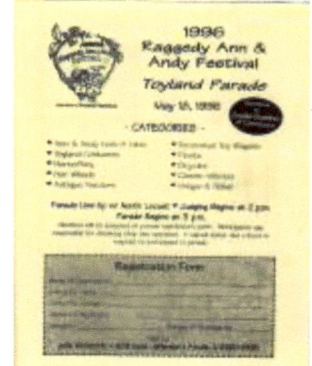

MANUFACTURER/MARKING

ITEM

Advertisement - 1997 Raggedy Ann and Andy Festival Toyland Parade Registration Form

SIZE

8½ x 11

MANUFACTURER/MARKING

May 17, 1997

ITEM

Advertisement - 1999 Holiday Keepsake Doll, Raggedy Ann

SIZE

8½ x 11

MANUFACTURER/MARKING

© Johnny Gruelle XMAS-4-99

ITEM

Advertisement - 1999 Raggedy Ann and Andy Festival Toyland Parade Registration Form

SIZE

8½ x 11

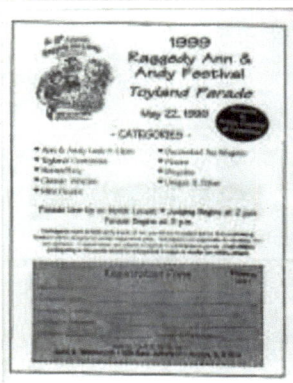

MANUFACTURER/MARKING

May 22, 1999

ITEM	SIZE
Advertisement - 2000 Raggedy Ann and Andy Festival Toyland Parade Registration Form	8½ x 11

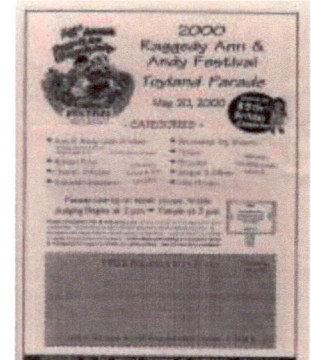

MANUFACTURER/MARKING
May 20, 2000, Julia A. Woolworth

ITEM	SIZE
Advertisement - 2001 Raggedy Ann and Andy Festival Toyland Parade Registration Form	8½ x 11

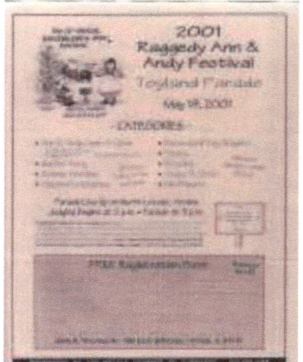

MANUFACTURER/MARKING
May 19, 2001

ITEM	SIZE
Advertisement - 2001 United Media Licensing Raggedy Ann and Raggedy Andy	7½ x 11

MANUFACTURER/MARKING
Simon & Schuster, Inc., United Media

ITEM	SIZE
Advertisement - 2002 Raggedy Ann and Andy Festival Toyland Parade Registration Form	8½ x 11

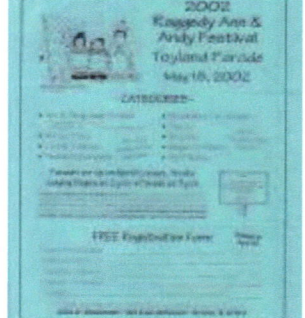

MANUFACTURER/MARKING
May 18, 2002

ITEM

Advertisement - 2003 Original Raggedy Ann and Andy Festival Parade Waiver and Release

SIZE

8½ x 11

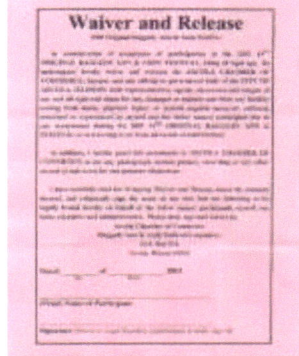

MANUFACTURER/MARKING

ITEM

Advertisement - 2003 Raggedy Ann and Andy Festival Parade Registration Form

SIZE

8½ x 11

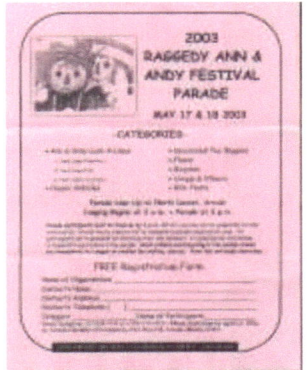

MANUFACTURER/MARKING

May 17 and 18, 2003

ITEM

Advertisement - 2003 United Media Licensing Raggedy Ann and Raggedy Andy

SIZE

8½ x 11

MANUFACTURER/MARKING

© Simon & Schuster, Inc., licensed by United Media, Lindsay Martinez

ITEM

Advertisement - 2004 Raggedy Ann and Andy Festival Parade Registration Form

SIZE

8½ x 11

MANUFACTURER/MARKING

May 22nd at 3:00 p.m.

ITEM

Advertisement - 2004 United Media Licensing Raggedy Ann and Raggedy Andy

SIZE

8½ x 11

MANUFACTURER/MARKING

Simon & Schuster, Inc., United Media, Lindsay Martinez

ITEM

Advertisement - 2005 Raggedy Ann and Andy Festival Toyland Parade Registration Form

SIZE

8½ x 11

MANUFACTURER/MARKING

May 21st at 3:00 p.m.

ITEM

Advertisement - 2006 Christmas Spectacular Starring The Rockettes

SIZE

6 x 9

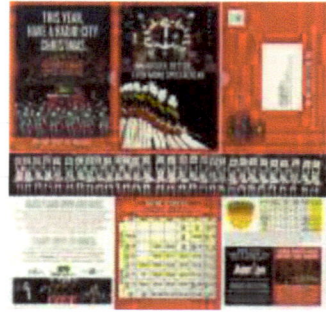

MANUFACTURER/MARKING

Hallmark Channel, North Fork Bank, American Express

ITEM

Advertisement - 2006 Raggedy Ann and Andy Festival Toyland Parade Registration Form

SIZE

8½ x 11

MANUFACTURER/MARKING

June 10th at 3:00 p.m.

ITEM

Advertisement - 2006 United Media Licensing Raggedy Ann and Raggedy Andy

SIZE

8½ x 11

MANUFACTURER/MARKING

Simon & Schuster, Inc., United Media, Sherikay Perry

ITEM

Advertisement - 2007 Raggedy Ann and Andy Festival Toyland Parade Registration Form

SIZE

8½ x 11

MANUFACTURER/MARKING

June 9th at 3:00 p.m.

ITEM

Advertisement - 2007-2008 United Media Licensing Raggedy Ann and Me!

SIZE

8½ x 11

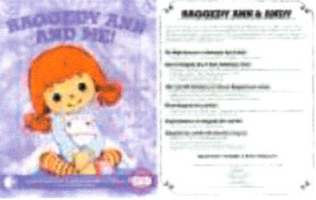

MANUFACTURER/MARKING

Simon & Schuster, Inc., licensed by United Media

ITEM

Advertisement - 2008 United Media Licensing Raggedy Ann and Raggedy Andy

SIZE

8½ x 11

MANUFACTURER/MARKING

© Simon & Schuster, Inc., licensed by United Media, Sherikay Perry

ITEM

Advertisement - 2009 United Media Licensing Raggedy Ann and Me!

SIZE

8½ x 11

MANUFACTURER/MARKING

Simon & Schuster, Inc., United Media, Sherikay Perry

ITEM

Advertisement - 2022 Raggedy Ann Rally Schedule of Events

SIZE

8½ x 11

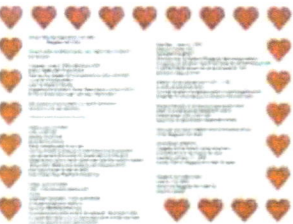

MANUFACTURER/MARKING

ITEM

Advertisement - 25 inch Walking Dolls

SIZE

8⅛ x 11

MANUFACTURER/MARKING

1974 Spiegel

ITEM

Advertisement - 25" Raggedy Ann and Andy dolls made by the Blue Ridge Hearthside Crafts Cooperative

SIZE

6 x 9

MANUFACTURER/MARKING

ITEM	SIZE
Advertisement - 3-in-1 stowaway and toy toter	8⅛ x 11

MANUFACTURER/MARKING
1974 Spiegel

ITEM	SIZE
Advertisement - 3rd Annual Florida Raggedy Ann, Doll and Teddy Bear Convention	8½ x 11

MANUFACTURER/MARKING
Joni Gruelle, Simon & Schuster, Inc., January 28-29, 2000

ITEM	SIZE
Advertisement - 3rd Annual Florida Raggedy Ann, Doll and Teddy Bear Convention	8½ x 11

MANUFACTURER/MARKING
January 28 and 29, 2000

ITEM	SIZE
Advertisement - 5K North Trail for 2004	8½ x 11

 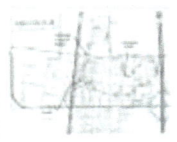

MANUFACTURER/MARKING

ITEM	SIZE
Advertisement - 5K North Trail for 2007	8½ x 11

MANUFACTURER/MARKING

ITEM	SIZE
Advertisement - 5K North Trail for 2008	8½ x 11

MANUFACTURER/MARKING

19th Raggedy Ann and Andy Festival, June 14, 2008

ITEM	SIZE
Advertisement - 5K North Trail for 2011	8½ x 11

MANUFACTURER/MARKING

ITEM	SIZE
Advertisement - 5K North Trail for 2012	8½ x 11

MANUFACTURER/MARKING

Raggedy Ann and Andy Friendship Gathering June 2 and Walldogs June 24, 2012

ITEM	SIZE
Advertisement - 5K South Trail for 2005	8½ x 11

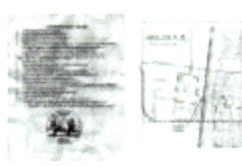

MANUFACTURER/MARKING

ITEM	SIZE
Advertisement - 5K South Trail for 2006	8½ x 11

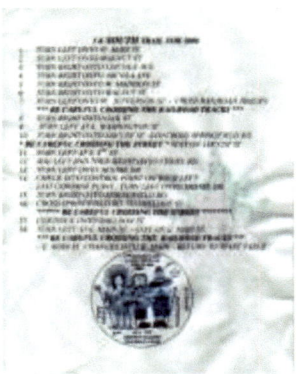

MANUFACTURER/MARKING

17th Raggedy Ann and Andy Festival, Arcola, Illinois

ITEM	SIZE
Advertisement - 5K South Trail for 2008	8½ x 11

MANUFACTURER/MARKING

19th Raggedy Ann and Andy Festival, June 14, 2008

ITEM	SIZE
Advertisement - 5K South Trail for 2011	8½ x 11

MANUFACTURER/MARKING

ITEM

Advertisement - 5K South Trail for 2012

SIZE

8½ x 11

MANUFACTURER/MARKING

Raggedy Ann and Andy Friendship Gathering June 2 and Walldogs, June 24, 2012, Advertisement says 5K South Trail for 2011. It is a typo. See previous description/picture for 2011.

ITEM

Advertisement - 5th Annual Raggedy Ann and Andy Festival

SIZE

5½ x 8½

MANUFACTURER/MARKING

May 21 and 22, 1994, Arcola, Illinois, birthplace of Johnny Gruelle

ITEM

Advertisement - 5th Annual Raggedy Ann and Andy Gospel Music Concert

SIZE

5½ x 8½

MANUFACTURER/MARKING

Sunday, May 22, 1994, Arcola, Illinois

ITEM

Advertisement - 5th Annual Raggedy Friendship Gathering

SIZE

8½ x 11

MANUFACTURER/MARKING

ITEM	SIZE
Advertisement - 5th Raggedy Ann and Andy Walk (Volksmarch)	5½ x 8½

MANUFACTURER/MARKING	
May 21, 2005, 8:00 a.m.	

ITEM	SIZE
Advertisement - 6th Ohio and Surrounding States Raggedy Gathering	8½ x 11

MANUFACTURER/MARKING	
Saturday, July 31, 2004, 12:00	

ITEM	SIZE
Advertisement - 7 Lovable Red Haired Rag Dolls	10¼ x 13⅛

MANUFACTURER/MARKING	
1971 Greenland Studios	

ITEM	SIZE
Advertisement - 70 Years Young Certificate of Authenticity	5 x 7

MANUFACTURER/MARKING	
Flambro Imports, Inc., 1,363 of 2,500	

ITEM	SIZE
Advertisement - 8th Annual Raggedy Ann Festival and Raggedy Ann 5K Run	8½ x 11

MANUFACTURER/MARKING

April 17, 2010

ITEM	SIZE
Advertisement - 8th Raggedy Ann and Andy Walk (Volksmarch)	5½ x 8½

MANUFACTURER/MARKING

Ridgewalkers Walking Club

ITEM	SIZE
Advertisement - 90 Years Ago: All Dolled Up	8½ x 11

MANUFACTURER/MARKING

Smithsonian, September 2005

ITEM	SIZE
Advertisement - 90th Anniversary Raggedy Ann and Andy Commemorative Dolls Certificate of Authenticity, Raggedy Andy	5 x 7

MANUFACTURER/MARKING

Joni Gruelle, Russ Berrie & Co., Inc.

ITEM	SIZE
Advertisement - 90th Anniversary Raggedy Ann and Andy Commemorative Dolls Certificate of Authenticity, Raggedy Ann	5 x 7

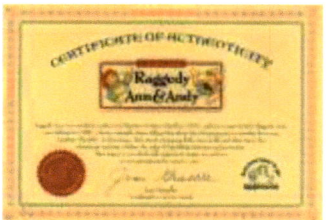

MANUFACTURER/MARKING
Joni Gruelle, Russ Berrie & Co., Inc.

ITEM	SIZE
Advertisement - A Book Update from Patty Hall	8½ x 11

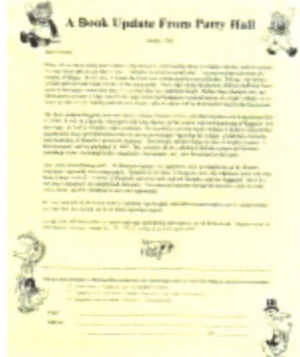

MANUFACTURER/MARKING

ITEM	SIZE
Advertisement - A Century of Dolls	8½ x 11

MANUFACTURER/MARKING
Karen D'Onobrio

ITEM	SIZE
Advertisement - A Chore is Fun When Done for a Friend Certificate of Authenticity	3¼ x 7⅜

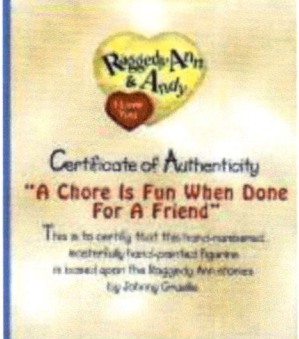

MANUFACTURER/MARKING
Simon & Schuster, Inc., licensed by United Media, Enesco Corp. 045544389341 288969

ITEM

Advertisement - A Collection of Childhood Antiques Including an American Novelties Ann

SIZE

4¾ x 7½

MANUFACTURER/MARKING

ITEM

Advertisement - A Cup of Friendship Warms the Heart Certificate of Authenticity

SIZE

3¼ x 7⅜

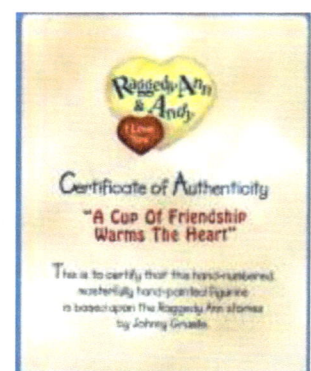

MANUFACTURER/MARKING

Simon & Schuster, Inc., licensed by United Media, Enesco Corp. 045544238168 823466

ITEM

Advertisement - A Friend from Knickerbocker

SIZE

11 x 16¼

MANUFACTURER/MARKING

1978 Knickerbocker Toy Company, Inc., Remember when you were little and needed somebody to talk to? That's why we make friends.

ITEM

Advertisement - A Friend in Need is a Friend in Deed Certificate of Authenticity

SIZE

3¼ x 7⅜

MANUFACTURER/MARKING

Simon & Schuster, Inc., Licensed by United Media, Enesco Corp. 783668 04554464307

ITEM

Advertisement - A Good Companion Makes the Day Brighter Certificate of Authenticity

SIZE

3¼ x 7⅜

MANUFACTURER/MARKING

Simon & Schuster, Inc., licensed by United Media, Enesco Corp. 045544470377 864773

ITEM

Advertisement - A Heart Full of Happiness Certificate of Authenticity

SIZE

3¼ x 7⅜

MANUFACTURER/MARKING

Simon & Schuster, Inc., Enesco Corp. 045544649094 640506

ITEM

Advertisement - A Melody is a Memory in Our Hearts Certificate of Authenticity

SIZE

3¼ x 7⅛

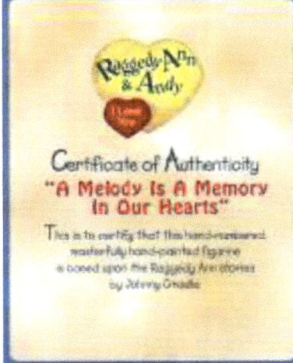

MANUFACTURER/MARKING

Simon & Schuster, Inc., licensed by United Media, Enesco Corp. 045544470834 864935

ITEM

Advertisement - A New Video from Sirocco Productions, Inc., Raggedy Ann and Andy: Johnny Gruelle's Dolls with Heart

SIZE

5½ x 8½

MANUFACTURER/MARKING

Sirocco Productions, Inc.

ITEM	SIZE
Advertisement - A Special Gift Brings a World of Smiles Certificate of Authenticity	3¼ x 7⅜

MANUFACTURER/MARKING
Simon & Schuster, Inc., licensed by United Media, Enesco Corp. 045544470490 864838

ITEM	SIZE
Advertisement - A Sprinkle of Love Makes Friendship Grow Certificate of Authenticity	3¼ x 7⅜

MANUFACTURER/MARKING
Simon & Schuster, Inc., licensed by United Media, Enesco Corp. 106218 045544550406

ITEM	SIZE
Advertisement - A Tasty Treat for a Friend So Sweet Certificate of Authenticity	3¼ x 7⅜

MANUFACTURER/MARKING
Simon & Schuster, Inc., licensed by United Media, Enesco Corp. 045544150897 823503

ITEM	SIZE
Advertisement - A Trunk Full of Treasures Certificate of Authenticity	3¼ x 7⅜

MANUFACTURER/MARKING
Simon & Schuster, Inc., licensed by United Media, Enesco Corp. 045544484589 868701

ITEM	SIZE
Advertisement - Alka-Seltzer	10 x 13

MANUFACTURER/MARKING
December 22, 1958 - Life

ITEM	SIZE
Advertisement - All Aboard the Friendship Express Certificate of Authenticity	3¼ x 7⅜

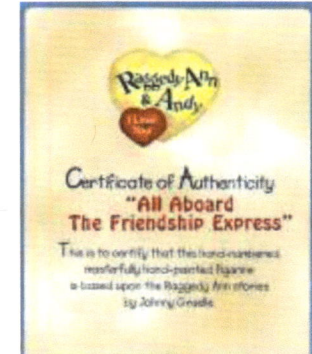

MANUFACTURER/MARKING
Simon & Schuster, Inc., licensed by United Media, Enesco Corp. 045544470483 864811

ITEM	SIZE
Advertisement - All Hearts Come Home at Christmas Certificate of Authenticity	3¼ x 7⅜

MANUFACTURER/MARKING
1999 Simon & Schuster, Inc., Enesco Corp. 597422 93RA001

ITEM	SIZE
Advertisement - All-steel kitchen	8⅛ x 11

MANUFACTURER/MARKING
1974 Spiegel

ITEM

Advertisement - Amazing Arcola, Amish Community, Raggedy Ann Historic Train Depot, Broom Sales

SIZE

3 x 7

MANUFACTURER/MARKING

ITEM

Advertisement - Amazing Arcola, An American Tradition

SIZE

9 x 12

MANUFACTURER/MARKING

Arcola Chamber of Commerce

ITEM

Advertisement - Amazing Arcola, Close to home away from it all

SIZE

8½ x 11

MANUFACTURER/MARKING

Arcola Chamber of Commerce

ITEM

Advertisement - Amazing Arcola, Discover Central Illinois, The 17th Original Raggedy Ann and Andy Festival

SIZE

8½ x 11

MANUFACTURER/MARKING

Just 2.5 hours from Chicago or St. Louis

ITEM	SIZE
Advertisement - Amazing Arcola, Raggedy Ann and Andy in front of a horse drawn carriage, Raggedy Andy is holding a broom, purple background	3 x 7

MANUFACTURER/MARKING

ITEM	SIZE
Advertisement - America Grows…America	6⅝ x 10

MANUFACTURER/MARKING

U.S. Keds The Shoe of Champions

ITEM	SIZE
Advertisement - American Country Fair	8⅜ x 11¾

MANUFACTURER/MARKING

November 4-10, 2003 © Simon & Schuster, Inc., Licensed by United Media, www.umkki.co.jp/raggedy

ITEM	SIZE
Advertisement - American Jazz Antiques	5¾ x 6½

MANUFACTURER/MARKING

Menage a Trois?

ITEM	SIZE
Advertisement - Andy by Kelly RuBert	11 x 14

MANUFACTURER/MARKING

1996 Hasbro, Inc.

ITEM	SIZE
Advertisement - Andy by Kelly RuBert Certificate of Ownership	4½ x 6½

MANUFACTURER/MARKING

1997 Hasbro, Inc., The Danbury Mint D575

ITEM	SIZE
Advertisement - Andy by Kelly RuBert Posing Instructions	5½ x 8½

MANUFACTURER/MARKING

Andy, 2/PC, c MBI

ITEM	SIZE
Advertisement - Ann by Kelly RuBert Certificate of Ownership	4½ x 6½

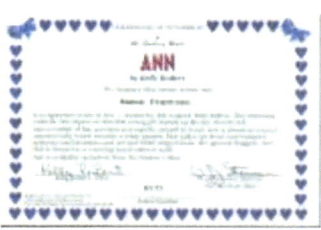

MANUFACTURER/MARKING
1996 Hasbro, Inc., The Danbury Mint D575

ITEM	SIZE
Advertisement - Ann by Kelly RuBert Posing Instructions	5½ x 8½

MANUFACTURER/MARKING
Ann, 1/PC, c MBI

ITEM	SIZE
Advertisement - Ann by Kelly RuBert; All dressed up like her favorite doll	14½ x 17

MANUFACTURER/MARKING
1996 Hasbro, Inc., The Danbury Mint

ITEM	SIZE
Advertisement - Ann by Kelly RuBert; All dressed up like her favorite doll Reservation Application	5½ x 10⅜

MANUFACTURER/MARKING
1996 Hasbro, Inc., The Danbury Mint

ITEM

Advertisement - Annual Raggedy Ann and Andy Ornament Collection Reservation Application

SIZE

3⅜ x 5⅝

MANUFACTURER/MARKING

008550 1 J540 1/1 AAA 318

ITEM

Advertisement - Any cereal my family leaves is first choice with me as long as it's in Post-Tens

SIZE

9⅞ x 13¼

MANUFACTURER/MARKING

General Foods, Dick Sargent

ITEM

Advertisement - Any choice of cereals tempts any family as long as it's from Post-Tens

SIZE

10 x 11¼

MANUFACTURER/MARKING

General Foods, Dick Sargent

ITEM

Advertisement - Applause 1998 Merchandise, including Dance with Me Dolls

SIZE

8½ x 11

MANUFACTURER/MARKING

1998 Applause, Inc., © Johnny Gruelle RAG-6-98

ITEM	SIZE
Advertisement - Applause 8", 12", 25" and 36" Dolls from The Last Great Company	8½ x 11

MANUFACTURER/MARKING
© 96 The Last Great Co.

ITEM	SIZE
Advertisement - Applause Beanbags and Fashion Gift Set	8½ x 11

MANUFACTURER/MARKING
RAG-6-98

ITEM	SIZE
Advertisement - Applause Box Set with certificate of authenticity	8½ x 11

MANUFACTURER/MARKING

ITEM	SIZE
Advertisement - Applause Classic Dolls, 12"-36"	8½ x 11

MANUFACTURER/MARKING
1988 Macmillan, Inc.

ITEM | SIZE
Advertisement - Applause Classic Dolls, 8"-48" | 8½ x 11

MANUFACTURER/MARKING

1988 Macmillan, Inc.

ITEM | SIZE
Advertisement - Applause Classic Dolls, 8, 12, 12 (brown), 17, 25 and 36 inch and Country | 11 x 17

MANUFACTURER/MARKING

RAG-6-98

ITEM | SIZE
Advertisement - Applause Display Fixture, Classic Dolls and Denim Dolls | 8½ x 11

MANUFACTURER/MARKING

1989 Johnny Gruelle Co., Macmillan, Inc.

ITEM | SIZE
Advertisement - Applause Exposition Company Reproduction Dolls | 8½ x 11

MANUFACTURER/MARKING

Raggedys and Teddys Co.

ITEM	SIZE
Advertisement - Applause Exposition Company Reproduction Dolls	11 x 17

MANUFACTURER/MARKING
RAG-1-98

ITEM	SIZE
Advertisement - Applause Presents an American Tradition	8½ x 11

MANUFACTURER/MARKING

ITEM	SIZE
Advertisement - Applause Raggedy Ann and Andy Doll and Book Sets	11 x 17

MANUFACTURER/MARKING
RAG-6-98

ITEM	SIZE
Advertisement - Applause Rags Raggedy Ann and Andy	8½ x 11

MANUFACTURER/MARKING
RAG-6-98

ITEM	SIZE
Advertisement - Applause Tea for Two Set and Talking Raggedy Ann	8½ x 11

MANUFACTURER/MARKING
RAG-6-98

ITEM	SIZE
Advertisement - Arcola Emporium	8½ x 14

MANUFACTURER/MARKING
201 East Main Street, Arcola, Illinois 61910

ITEM	SIZE
Advertisement - Arcola Here We Come, The 17th Original Raggedy Ann and Andy Festival, Patty Hall and her Musical Performances	8½ x 11

MANUFACTURER/MARKING
Arcola, Illinois, Friday, Saturday, Sunday, June 9-10-11, 2006

ITEM	SIZE
Advertisement - Arcola Record-Herald 1999 Raggedy Ann Issue	5⅜ x 8½

MANUFACTURER/MARKING
Rankin Publishing Co., Inc.

ITEM

Advertisement - Arcola Record-Herald Raggedy Ann and Andy Festival, 2002 issue order form

SIZE

8½ x 11

MANUFACTURER/MARKING

ITEM

Advertisement - Arcola Record-Herald Raggedy Ann and Andy Festival, May 24, 2001 issue order form

SIZE

8½ x 11

MANUFACTURER/MARKING

ITEM

Advertisement - Arcola Record-Herald Raggedy Ann and Andy Festival, May 25, 2000 issue order form

SIZE

6½ x 9

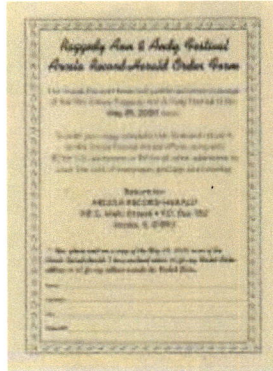

MANUFACTURER/MARKING

ITEM

Advertisement - Arcola's 6th Annual Raggedy Ann and Andy Festival

SIZE

5½ x 8½

MANUFACTURER/MARKING

May 20 and 21, 1995, Arcola, Illinois, birthplace of Johnny Gruelle

ITEM | SIZE
Advertisement - Arcola's 7th Annual Raggedy Ann and Andy Festival | 5½ x 8½

MANUFACTURER/MARKING

May 18 and 19, 1996, Arcola, Illinois, birthplace of Johnny Gruelle

ITEM | SIZE
Advertisement - Arcola's Raggedy Ann and Andy Cross Stitch Pre-event | 8½ x 11

MANUFACTURER/MARKING

Thursday, June 6, 2002

ITEM | SIZE
Advertisement - Are You Listening to What Your Child May Not Be Saying? | 3½ x 8½

MANUFACTURER/MARKING

1985 Macmillan, Inc., National Easter Seal Society PR-31

ITEM | SIZE
Advertisement - At Christmas My Heart Thinks of You Certificate of Authenticity | 3¼ x 7⅜

MANUFACTURER/MARKING

Simon & Schuster, Inc., licensed by United Media, Enesco Corp. 045544272827 104402

ITEM | SIZE
Advertisement - Aveda Skin Care and Color Cosmetics | 7⅝ x 10¾

MANUFACTURER/MARKING

Ever wonder why some shampoo makes your hair feel like yarn?

ITEM | SIZE
Advertisement - Baby Andy by Kelly RuBert Certificate of Ownership | 4½ x 6½

MANUFACTURER/MARKING

1988 Hasbro, Inc., The Danbury Mint A822

ITEM | SIZE
Advertisement - Baby Andy by Kelly RuBert Posing Instructions | 5½ x 8½

MANUFACTURER/MARKING

1988 Hasbro, Inc., RAB, 1/PC, c MBI

ITEM | SIZE
Advertisement - Baby Annie by Kelly RuBert Certificate of Ownership | 4½ x 6½

MANUFACTURER/MARKING

1998 Hasbro, Inc., by Kelly RuBert A822

ITEM | SIZE
Advertisement - Baby Annie by Kelly RuBert Posing Instructions | 5½ x 8½

MANUFACTURER/MARKING
1988 Hasbro, Inc., RAB, 1/PC, c MBI

ITEM | SIZE
Advertisement - Backyard play area | 4⅞ x 7⅞

MANUFACTURER/MARKING

ITEM | SIZE
Advertisement - Banks | 8⅛ x 11

MANUFACTURER/MARKING
1974 The Bobbs-Merrill Co., Inc., J.C. Penney

ITEM | SIZE
Advertisement - Banquet and Silent Auction Information | 8½ x 11

MANUFACTURER/MARKING
Johnny Mouse

ITEM	SIZE
Advertisement - Banquet and Silent Auction Information	8½ x 11

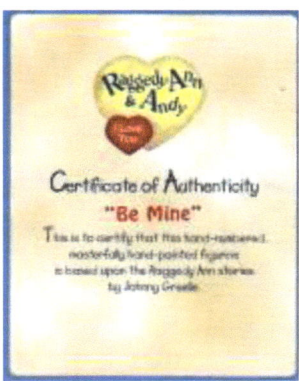

MANUFACTURER/MARKING

King Chocolate Drop

ITEM	SIZE
Advertisement - Be Mine Certificate of Authenticity	3¼ x 7⅜

MANUFACTURER/MARKING

Simon & Schuster, Inc., Enesco Corp. 045544649070 640484

ITEM	SIZE
Advertisement - Beanbag Raggedy Ann and Andy and 25 and 31 inch tall Raggedy Ann and Andy	8⅛ x 22

MANUFACTURER/MARKING

1974 Spiegel

ITEM	SIZE
Advertisement - Bedroom Coordinates	8⅛ x 11

MANUFACTURER/MARKING

1974 The Bobbs-Merrill Co., Inc., J.C. Penney

ITEM

Advertisement - Bedroom Ensemble

SIZE

8⅛ x 11

MANUFACTURER/MARKING

1974 Spiegel

ITEM

Advertisement - Being Nine is Really Fine Certificate of Authenticity

SIZE

3¼ x 7⅜

MANUFACTURER/MARKING

Simon & Schuster, Inc., licensed by United Media, Enesco Corp. 045544229340 823813

ITEM

Advertisement - Better Homes & Gardens

SIZE

9¾ x 12⅝

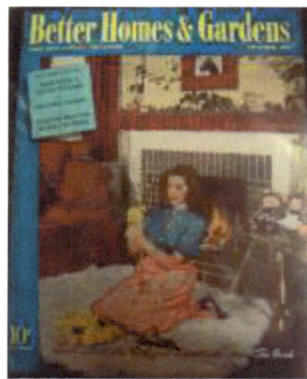

MANUFACTURER/MARKING

November 1941

ITEM

Advertisement - Betty Crocker Storybook Dinnerware

SIZE

7¾ x 10¾

MANUFACTURER/MARKING

Women's Day 1970-71

ITEM	SIZE
Advertisement - Birthday Surprise Certificate of Authenticity	3¾ x 6¾

MANUFACTURER/MARKING
1999 Simon & Schuster, Inc., The Danbury Mint A807, Peter B. Maglathlin, Director

ITEM	SIZE
Advertisement - Birthdays Are Full of Surprises Certificate of Authenticity	3¼ x 7⅜

MANUFACTURER/MARKING
Simon & Schuster, Inc., licensed by United Media, Enesco Corp. 045544151566 823856

ITEM	SIZE
Advertisement - Black and Decker, Raggedy Ann propped up on a pillow, without logo	7⅛ x 10½

MANUFACTURER/MARKING
Some gifts become even more appreciated as time passes

ITEM	SIZE
Advertisement - Black and Decker, Raggedy Ann propped upon a pillow, with logo	7⅛ x 10½

MANUFACTURER/MARKING
Some gifts become even more appreciated as time passes

ITEM	SIZE
Advertisement - Blue Cross returns 93 cents of every dollar in actual hospital care	10¼ x 13½

MANUFACTURER/MARKING

Blue Cross Association, 840 North Lake Shore Drive, Chicago 11, Illinois, Saturday Evening Post

ITEM	SIZE
Advertisement - Broadway Palm Children's Theatre	8½ x 11

MANUFACTURER/MARKING

2000

ITEM	SIZE
Advertisement - Bumpy Roads are Easier When We Are Happy Inside Certificate of Authenticity	3¼ x 7⅜

MANUFACTURER/MARKING

1999 Simon & Schuster, Inc., Enesco Corp. 544884 93RA672

ITEM	SIZE
Advertisement - Cake Decorations, Happy Birthday	5½ x 8⅛

MANUFACTURER/MARKING

1980 Bobbs-Merrill Co., Inc. 301, 1984 The Lucks Co. Fast Finish

ITEM

Advertisement - Calendar of Events for 2003

SIZE

5½ x 8½

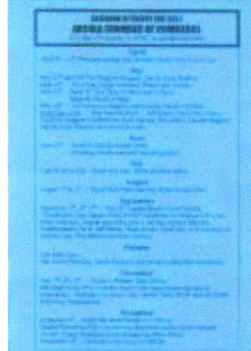

MANUFACTURER/MARKING

Arcola Chamber of Commerce

ITEM

Advertisement - Camel with the Wrinkled Knees Certificate of Authenticity

SIZE

3½ x 5⅜

MANUFACTURER/MARKING

#134/350 R. John Wright Dolls, Inc., Bennington, VT, Simon & Schuster, Inc., licensed by United Media

ITEM

Advertisement - Camel with the Wrinkled Knees Registration Card

SIZE

3⅜ x 5¼

MANUFACTURER/MARKING

#134/350 R. John Wright Dolls, Inc., Bennington, VT, Simon & Schuster, Inc., licensed by United Media

ITEM

Advertisement - Canada Dry

SIZE

11 x 14

MANUFACTURER/MARKING

1954

ITEM

Advertisement - Caring for You When You're Blue Certificate of Authenticity

SIZE

3¼ x 7⅜

MANUFACTURER/MARKING

Simon & Schuster, Inc., licensed by United Media, Enesco Corp. 045544391313 290394

ITEM

Advertisement - Carter's Permanent Markers, Mark it. For keeps.

SIZE

4½ x 4½ x 4½

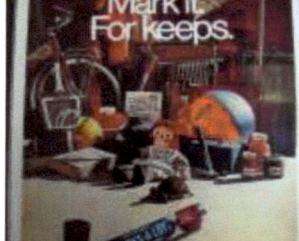

MANUFACTURER/MARKING

Carter's Ink Co., Cambridge, Massachusetts 02142

ITEM

Advertisement - Cast a Smile, Catch Some Joy Certificate of Authenticity

SIZE

3¼ x 7⅜

MANUFACTURER/MARKING

Simon & Schuster, Inc., licensed by United Media, Enesco Corp. 045544679749 677701

ITEM

Advertisement - Catch a Little Summer Fun Certificate of Authenticity

SIZE

3¼ x 7⅜

MANUFACTURER/MARKING

Simon & Schuster, Inc., licensed by United Media, Enesco Corp. 045544679800 677779

ITEM	SIZE
Advertisement - Categories for Luncheon Competition and Competition Entry Form	8½ x 11

MANUFACTURER/MARKING
Mary D'Angelo

ITEM	SIZE
Advertisement - Ceramic Figurine Maker	8½ x 11

MANUFACTURER/MARKING
1974 Spiegel

ITEM	SIZE
Advertisement - Cheery Scarecrow with button centerpiece raffle	4¼ x 5

MANUFACTURER/MARKING
This button posy which you see, is a bid for the table decoration to be

ITEM	SIZE
Advertisement - Children's Favorite Dolls and Puppets	8¼ x 10⅞

MANUFACTURER/MARKING
1977 National Catalog Showrooms

ITEM | SIZE
Advertisement - Children's Miracle Network | 8½ x 11

MANUFACTURER/MARKING
Quad Marketing

ITEM | SIZE
Advertisement - Children's Miracle Network Telethon | 5 x 7⅜

MANUFACTURER/MARKING
Invest in a small miracle, New York Hospital-Cornell Medical Center

ITEM | SIZE
Advertisement - Christmas with Raggedy Ann and Andy | 11 x 14

MANUFACTURER/MARKING
Simon & Schuster, Inc., licensed by United Media, MBIX RD/bro

ITEM | SIZE
Advertisement - Christmas with Raggedy Ann and Andy Certificate of Authenticity | 3⅝ x 6

MANUFACTURER/MARKING
Simon & Schuster, Inc., licensed by United Media, Peter B. Maglathlin, Director A1744

ITEM

Advertisement - Christmas with Raggedy Ann and Andy Posing Instructions

SIZE

4¼ x 8½

MANUFACTURER/MARKING

7018/1/UPC

ITEM

Advertisement - Christmas with Raggedy Ann and Andy Reservation Application

SIZE

5½ x 8½

MANUFACTURER/MARKING

Simon & Schuster, Inc., licensed by United Media, XRD/ocr

ITEM

Advertisement - Cold Hands, Warm Heart Certificate of Authenticity

SIZE

3¼ x 7⅜

MANUFACTURER/MARKING

1999 Simon & Schuster, Inc., Enesco Corp. 597449 92RA542

ITEM

Advertisement - Come live in the electric climate - The air is so clean there, Edison Institute

SIZE

10¼ x 13

MANUFACTURER/MARKING

ITEM	SIZE
Advertisement - Cookies are for Sharing, Hearts are For Caring Certificate of Authenticity	3¼ x 7⅜

MANUFACTURER/MARKING
Simon & Schuster, Inc., licensed by United Media, Enesco Corp. 045544272919 104409

ITEM	SIZE
Advertisement - Cottage, Raggedy Ann and Raggedy Arthur purse with snap, camper, car and doghouse	7⅞ x 10⅞

MANUFACTURER/MARKING
Aldens Christmas Catalog 1981

ITEM	SIZE
Advertisement - Cover Girl, Raggedy Ann is Newsday's Christmas Almanac cover girl	2½ x 3⅞

MANUFACTURER/MARKING
Photo by Lee Levine

ITEM	SIZE
Advertisement - Crosley Broadcasting Corporation, She's A Doll...	10¼ x 12½

MANUFACTURER/MARKING
WLW-C, Columbus/WLW-I, Indianapolis/WLW-T, Cincinnati/WLW-D, Dayton/WLW Radio Cincinnati, A subsidiary of Avco

ITEM	SIZE
Advertisement - Cross My Heart, I'll Always be Your Friend Certificate of Authenticity	3¼ x 7⅜

MANUFACTURER/MARKING
Simon & Schuster, Inc., licensed by United Media, Enesco Corp. 045544390279 289752

ITEM	SIZE
Advertisement - Curtis Publishing Company	5⅜ x 5½

MANUFACTURER/MARKING
1941 Saturday Evening Post

ITEM	SIZE
Advertisement - Dakin Everyday Raggedy Bear 80th and 85th Birthday, Raggedy Ann and Andy Dolls	8½ x 11

MANUFACTURER/MARKING
Storybook Raggedy Ann and Storybook Raggedy Andy, Dakin Signature Collection

ITEM	SIZE
Advertisement - Dakin Halloween Raggedy Ann	8½ x 11

MANUFACTURER/MARKING
2000 Johnny Gruelle, Dakin Signature Collection DH-3-00 16731

ITEM

Advertisement - Dakin Raggedy Ann Keepsake and Christmas Raggedy Ann

SIZE

8½ x 11

MANUFACTURER/MARKING

2000 Applause, Inc., Dakin Signature Collection HC-3-00

ITEM

Advertisement - Dakin Signature Collection

SIZE

3 x 5

MANUFACTURER/MARKING

Collector dolls based on Johnny Gruelle's original storybook characters

ITEM

Advertisement - Dakin Storybook Ann The Golden Butterfly and Storybook Andy with a Wishing Stick

SIZE

8½ x 11

MANUFACTURER/MARKING

Dakin Signature Collection RAG-7-00, $69.95 for the pair plus $10.25 U.P.S.

ITEM

Advertisement - Dakin Storybook Raggedy Ann and the Lucky Penny

SIZE

8½ x 11

MANUFACTURER/MARKING

Dakin Signature Collection RAG-9-00

ITEM

Advertisement - Dakin Valentine Raggedy Ann

SIZE

8½ x 11

MANUFACTURER/MARKING

Dakin Signature Collection 16750

ITEM

Advertisement - Dakin, We're Celebrating Two Very Special Birthdays

SIZE

8½ x 11

MANUFACTURER/MARKING

ITEM

Advertisement - Dancin' Duo Certificate of Authenticity

SIZE

3¾ x 6¾

MANUFACTURER/MARKING

2000 Simon & Schuster, Inc., The Danbury Mint A807, Peter B. Maglathlin, Director

ITEM

Advertisement - Dinnerware by Oneida

SIZE

8½ x 11

MANUFACTURER/MARKING

Oneida, The Bobbs-Merrill Company, Inc. 7-74 0-167

ITEM

Advertisement - Do it for Grins

SIZE

2¾ x 10 5/16

MANUFACTURER/MARKING

Children's Hospitals

ITEM

Advertisement - Do It for Grins, book

SIZE

7⅜ x 10⅜

MANUFACTURER/MARKING

Children's Hospitals

ITEM

Advertisement - Do it for Grins, dog

SIZE

1¾ x 10⅜

MANUFACTURER/MARKING

Raggedy Ann Storybook or 10" puppy plush

ITEM

Advertisement - Do It for Grins, dolls

SIZE

7⅜ x 10⅜

MANUFACTURER/MARKING

Children's Hospitals

ITEM	SIZE
Advertisement - Do it for Grins, Raggedy Andy doll	1¾ x 10¾

MANUFACTURER/MARKING
Children's Hospitals

ITEM	SIZE
Advertisement - Dolls by Jerri	8½ x 11

MANUFACTURER/MARKING
Dolls by Jerri, Charlotte, North Carolina

ITEM	SIZE
Advertisement - Dolls, Sleeping Bags and Raggedy Ann Doll Carriage	8⅛ x 11

MANUFACTURER/MARKING
1974 The Bobbs-Merrill Co., Inc., J.C. Penney

ITEM	SIZE
Advertisement - Each Day is Filled With Love and Sunshine Certificate of Authenticity	3¼ x 7⅜

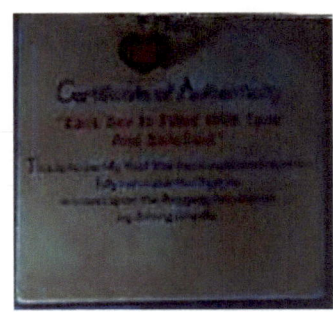

MANUFACTURER/MARKING
Simon & Schuster, Inc., Enesco Corp. 04554460427794RA760 544906

ITEM

Advertisement - Eight Decades of Love and Friendship

SIZE

9 x 12

MANUFACTURER/MARKING

ITEM

Advertisement - Eight to Eighty...Americans Just Naturally Love To Fly! More People Fly More Places by Douglas

SIZE

4½ x 4½ x 4½

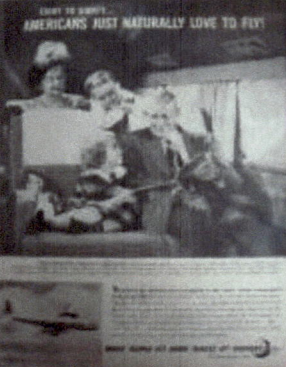

MANUFACTURER/MARKING

30th Anniversary Year - 1950

ITEM

Advertisement - Einstein, When Presents of Mind is Important

SIZE

8½ x 11

MANUFACTURER/MARKING

Don't forget to elevate to the E-MC 2nd Floor

ITEM

Advertisement - Elliott Erwitt, Raggedy Ann and Raggedy Andy sitting at a table with small Raggedy Ann and Raggedy Andy dolls on their plates

SIZE

10 x 11

MANUFACTURER/MARKING

December 1972 Life

ITEM	SIZE
Advertisement - Estate Sale Featuring Raggedy Ann and Andy Collectibles in Crete, Illinois	8½ x 11

MANUFACTURER/MARKING

www.susiesestates.com

ITEM	SIZE
Advertisement - Everyone Could Use a Helping Hand Certificate of Authenticity	3¼ x 7⅜

MANUFACTURER/MARKING

Simon & Schuster, Inc., licensed by United Media, Enesco Corp. 045544760171 953148

ITEM	SIZE
Advertisement - Everything Sounds Better When We Play Together	3¼ x 7⅛

MANUFACTURER/MARKING

Simon & Schuster, Inc., licensed by United Media, Enesco Corp. 045544471183 864951

ITEM	SIZE
Advertisement - Exposition Raggedy Ann and Raggedy Andy Dolls	8½ x 11

MANUFACTURER/MARKING

© Johnny Gruelle/Applause RAG-1-98

ITEM

Advertisement - Favorite Gift Certificate of Authenticity

SIZE

3 x 3⅞

MANUFACTURER/MARKING

Timeless Treasures, Vanmark 1, 0594

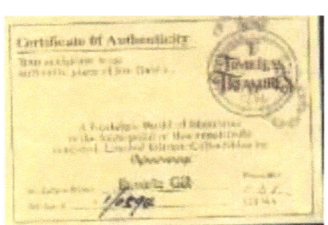

ITEM

Advertisement - Favorite Gift Registration of Ownership

SIZE

4 x 5¾

MANUFACTURER/MARKING

Timeless Treasures, Vanmark 1, 0594

ITEM

Advertisement - Filled to the Brim with Love Certificate of Authenticity

SIZE

3¼ x 7⅜

MANUFACTURER/MARKING

Simon & Schuster, Inc., licensed by United Media, Enesco Corp. 045544454253 823554

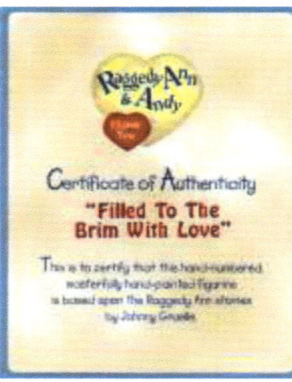

ITEM

Advertisement - First Annual Florida Raggedy Ann, Doll, and Teddy Bear Show, Sa e, and Luncheon

SIZE

8½ x 11

MANUFACTURER/MARKING

January 31, 1998 - Orlando, Florida

ITEM	SIZE
Advertisement - Fisher Price Pull Toy Certificate of Authenticity	3½ x 5⅝

MANUFACTURER/MARKING
3125

ITEM	SIZE
Advertisement - Flambro Figurines, An Old and Treasured American Classic is 70 Years Young, black and white	8½ x 11

MANUFACTURER/MARKING
1989 HC, Macmillan, Inc.

ITEM	SIZE
Advertisement - Flambro Figurines, An Old and Treasured American Classic is 70 Years Young, color	8½ x 11

MANUFACTURER/MARKING
1989, HC, Macmillan, Inc.

ITEM	SIZE
Advertisement - Flambro Lamps, Dish, Stocking Holder, Water Globe and Music Boxes	8½ x 11

MANUFACTURER/MARKING
1988 Macmillan, Inc.

ITEM	SIZE
Advertisement - Flambro Music Boxes and Six Statues	8½ x 11

MANUFACTURER/MARKING
1988 Macmillan, Inc.

ITEM	SIZE
Advertisement - Flambro Statues and Bookends	8½ x 11

MANUFACTURER/MARKING
1988 Macmillan, Inc.

ITEM	SIZE
Advertisement - Flambro Statues, Music Boxes and Ornaments	8½ x 11

MANUFACTURER/MARKING
1988 Macmillan, Inc.

ITEM	SIZE
Advertisement - Folding table and chairs, happy face rocker and child's dinette set	8½ x 22

MANUFACTURER/MARKING
1974 Spiegel

ITEM	SIZE
Advertisement - For You With My Heart's Best Love Certificate of Authenticity	3¼ x 7⅜

MANUFACTURER/MARKING
Simon & Schuster, Inc., Enesco Corp. 045544649056 640465

ITEM	SIZE
Advertisement - Forever Friends, Camel with the Wrinkled Knees Registration Card	3⅝ x 5¼

MANUFACTURER/MARKING
#304/350, R. John Wright Dolls, Inc., Bennington, VT, Simon & Schuster, Inc., licensed by United Media

ITEM	SIZE
Advertisement - Forever Friends, Camel with the Wrinkled Knees, miniature	6 x 8½

MANUFACTURER/MARKING
R. John Wright Dolls, Bennington, VT, Simon & Schuster, Inc., licensed by United Media

ITEM	SIZE
Advertisement - Forever Friends, Raggedy Ann and Andy	3 x 3½

MANUFACTURER/MARKING
R. John Wright, Simon & Schuster, Inc., licensed by United Media

ITEM	SIZE
Advertisement - Forever Friends, Raggedy Ann and Andy and the Camel with the Wrinkled Knees	2¾ x 4¼

MANUFACTURER/MARKING
R. John Wright, Simon & Schuster, Inc., licensed by United Media

ITEM	SIZE
Advertisement - Forever Friends, Raggedy Ann and Andy Certificate of Authenticity	3⅝ x 5⅝

MANUFACTURER/MARKING
#0497/1,000 R. John Wright Dolls, Inc., Bennington, VT, Simon & Schuster, Inc., licensed by United Media, Year of Issue: 2004

ITEM	SIZE
Advertisement - Forever Friends, Raggedy Ann and Andy, miniature	8½ x 11

MANUFACTURER/MARKING
The Toy Shoppe

ITEM	SIZE
Advertisement - Forever Friends, Raggedy Ann Camel with the Wrinkled Knees Certificate of Authenticity	2½ x 4

MANUFACTURER/MARKING
#304/350 R. John Wright Dolls, Inc., Bennington, VT, Simon & Schuster, Inc., licensed by United Media, Year of Issue: 2004

ITEM	SIZE
Advertisement - Forever Friends, The Little Brown Bear Certificate of Authenticity	2½ x 4

MANUFACTURER/MARKING
#233/350 R. John Wright Dolls, Inc., Bennington, VT, Simon & Schuster, Inc., licensed by United Media, Year of Issue: 2004

ITEM	SIZE
Advertisement - Forever Friends, The Little Brown Bear Registration Card	3⅝ x 5¼

MANUFACTURER/MARKING
#233/350 R. John Wright Dolls, Inc., Bennington, VT, Simon & Schuster, Inc., licensed by United Media, Year of Issue: 2004

ITEM	SIZE
Advertisement - Forever Friends, The Little Brown Bear Story	2¾ x 4¼

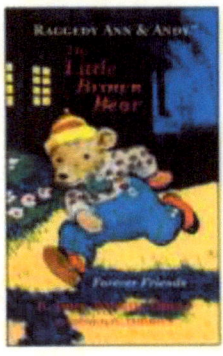

MANUFACTURER/MARKING
R. John Wright Dolls, Inc., Bennington, VT, Simon & Schuster, Inc., licensed by United Media

ITEM	SIZE
Advertisement - Forever Raggedy Ann and Andy Certificate of Authenticity	4½ x 6⅝

MANUFACTURER/MARKING
2011 Precious Moments, Inc., licensee, The Doll Maker, Sam Butcher #52/300

ITEM	SIZE
Advertisement - Forever True Certificate of Authenticity	3¼ x 7½

MANUFACTURER/MARKING
1999 Simon & Schuster, Inc., Enesco Corp. 544876 98RA517

ITEM	SIZE
Advertisement - Forever True Certificate of Authenticity	3¼ x 7½

MANUFACTURER/MARKING
1999 Simon & Schuster, Inc. #645958 Enesco Corporation #0431 of 3,000

ITEM	SIZE
Advertisement - Four Beloved Rag Doll Prints	11 x 17

MANUFACTURER/MARKING

ITEM	SIZE
Advertisement - Four Foot Graphics Kit Assembly Instructions	8½ x 11

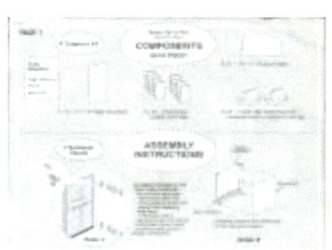

MANUFACTURER/MARKING
Item 878227

ITEM	SIZE
Advertisement - Free Parents' Guide to Raggedy Ann and Andy's Grow-and-Learn Library	7 x 8½

MANUFACTURER/MARKING

1988 Macmillan, Inc., Lynx Books

ITEM	SIZE
Advertisement - Friends Forever...No Matter the Weather Certificate of Authenticity	3¼ x 7⅜

MANUFACTURER/MARKING

Simon & Schuster, Inc., licensed by United Media, Enesco Corp. 045544711869 709042

ITEM	SIZE
Advertisement - Friends Like You Are a Special Treat Certificate of Authenticity	3¼ x 7⅜

MANUFACTURER/MARKING

Simon & Schuster, Inc., licensed by United Media, Enesco Corp. 04554463973 823422

ITEM	SIZE
Advertisement - Friends Like You Are Just Ducky Certificate of Authenticity	3¼ x 7⅜

MANUFACTURER/MARKING

Simon & Schuster, Inc., Enesco Corp. 04554460429194RA628 544922

ITEM	SIZE
Advertisement - Friendship is a Contract You Sign Certificate of Authenticity	3¼ x 7⅜

MANUFACTURER/MARKING
Simon & Schuster, Inc., licensed by United Media, Enesco Corp. 045544643 880783579

ITEM	SIZE
Advertisement - Friendship is My Special Tea Certificate of Authenticity	3¼ x 7⅜

MANUFACTURER/MARKING
Simon & Schuster, Inc., licensed by United Media, Enesco Corp. 045544662284 823473

ITEM	SIZE
Advertisement - Friendship is the Rhythm of Life Certificate of Authenticity	3¼ x 7⅜

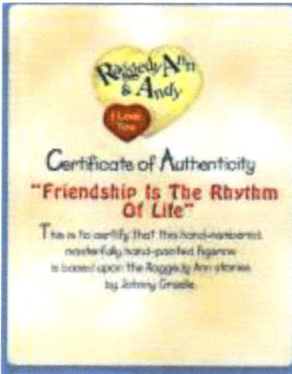

MANUFACTURER/MARKING
Simon & Schuster, Inc., licensed by United Media, Enesco Corp. 045544471176 864943

ITEM	SIZE
Advertisement - Friendship Makes it all Better Certificate of Authenticity	3¼ x 7⅜

MANUFACTURER/MARKING
Simon & Schuster, Inc., licensed by United Media, Enesco Corp. 045544760201 953164

ITEM

Advertisement - Friendship Warms the Heart and Soul Certificate of Authenticity

SIZE

3¼ x 7⅜

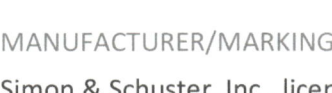

MANUFACTURER/MARKING

Simon & Schuster, Inc., licensed by United Media, Enesco Corp. 045544150880 823481

ITEM

Advertisement - Fun and Games Certificate of Authenticity

SIZE

3½ x 6⅞

MANUFACTURER/MARKING

1389C Anthony Marinatos, Managing Director, River Shore, James P. Smith, Jr., Chairman, The Hami Hon Collection

ITEM

Advertisement - Fun and Games Introduction Brochure

SIZE

7 x 7

MANUFACTURER/MARKING

The Hamilton Collection, 9550 Regency Square Boulevard, P.O. Box 2567, Jacksonville, FL 32232

ITEM

Advertisement - Fun and Games Trading Card

SIZE

3½ x 5

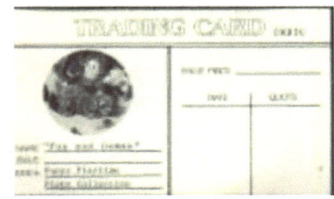

MANUFACTURER/MARKING

CN8TC

ITEM | SIZE
Advertisement - Fun Furniture | 8⅛ x 11

MANUFACTURER/MARKING

1974 The Bobbs-Merrill Co., Inc., J.C. Penney

ITEM | SIZE
Advertisement - Geoffrey Beene Wool Dress | 9⅞ x 13⅛

MANUFACTURER/MARKING

ITEM | SIZE
Advertisement - Georgia Rag Time | 8½ x 11

MANUFACTURER/MARKING

Saturday, July 28, 2001, 10-3 p.m., Macon, Georgia

ITEM | SIZE
Advertisement - Get Into the Halloween Spirit Certificate of Authenticity | 3¼ x 7⅜

MANUFACTURER/MARKING

Simon & Schuster, Inc., licensed by United Media/Enesco Group, Inc. 045544272735 104394

ITEM

Advertisement - Gift Toys to Bank On

SIZE

6⅜ x 10⅛

MANUFACTURER/MARKING

The Saturday Evening Post, October '74

ITEM

Advertisement - Gilbert Quality Papers, I'm glad we're made of more than sawdust

SIZE

11 x 14

MANUFACTURER/MARKING

Worth Gruelle

ITEM

Advertisement - Girl carrying Raggedy Ann while opening a door

SIZE

10 x 13

MANUFACTURER/MARKING

September 22, 1961 - Life

ITEM

Advertisement - Girl holding and surrounded by four McCall's homemade Raggedy Anns and one Raggedy Andy

SIZE

10¼ x 13

MANUFACTURER/MARKING

McCall's Pattern Co., 1970 The Bobbs-Merrill Co., Inc.

ITEM

Advertisement - GMAC Time Payment Plan

SIZE

9¾ x 12⅞

MANUFACTURER/MARKING

1961 The Saturday Evening Post

ITEM

Advertisement - Gold Seal Nairn Inlaid Linoleum

SIZE

10¼ x 13½

MANUFACTURER/MARKING

1952 Congoleum-Nairn, Inc.

ITEM

Advertisement - Golden Cockerel Russian Gifts

SIZE

8½ x 10

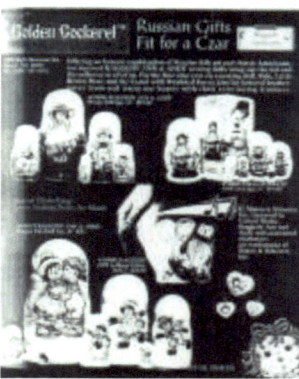

MANUFACTURER/MARKING

Simon & Schuster, Inc., licensed by United Media

ITEM

Advertisement - Good Deeds Fill the Heart with Joy Certificate of Authenticity

SIZE

3¼ x 7⅜

MANUFACTURER/MARKING

Simon & Schuster, Inc., licensed by United Media, Enesco Corp. 045544435345 100053

ITEM	SIZE
Advertisement - Greet the Season Oh So Jolly, with Mistletoe, Tinsel, Lights and...Certificate of Authenticity	3¼ x 7⅜

MANUFACTURER/MARKING
Simon & Schuster, Inc., licensed by United Media, Enesco Corp. 045544272797 104400

ITEM	SIZE
Advertisement - Guess the Number of Candy Hearts Entry Form	3 x 3¾

MANUFACTURER/MARKING
Actual number of candy hearts 952, 950 guessed by Robyn Amato

ITEM	SIZE
Advertisement - Halloween with Raggedy Ann and Andy Certificate of Authenticity	3⅝ x 6

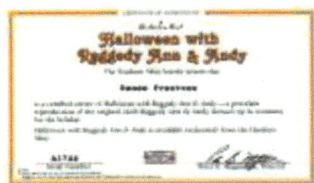

MANUFACTURER/MARKING
Simon & Schuster, Inc., licensed by United Media A1744, Peter B. Maglathlin, Director

ITEM	SIZE
Advertisement - Halloween with Raggedy Ann and Andy Option Form	3⅝ x 6

MANUFACTURER/MARKING
A1744, 7018/of

ITEM	SIZE
Advertisement - Halloween with Raggedy Ann and Andy Posing Instructions	4¼ x 8½

MANUFACTURER/MARKING
MBI 7018/2/UPC

ITEM	SIZE
Advertisement - Hand Crafted Nutcrackers	8½ x 11

MANUFACTURER/MARKING
Available October 2003

ITEM	SIZE
Advertisement - Handcrafted Nutcrackers Limited Edition Registration Card	4⅛ x 5⅞

MANUFACTURER/MARKING
Simon & Schuster, Inc., licensed by United Media

ITEM	SIZE
Advertisement - Happiness is a Birthday Shared with You Certificate of Authenticity	3¼ x 7⅜

MANUFACTURER/MARKING
Simon & Schuster, Inc., licensed by United Media, Enesco Corp. 045544151818 823821

ITEM	SIZE
Advertisement - Happiness is Homemade Certificate of Authenticity	3¼ x 7⅜

MANUFACTURER/MARKING
Simon & Schuster, Inc., licensed by United Media, Enesco Corp. 045544272810 104401

ITEM	SIZE
Advertisement - Happiness is Sharing a Cheery Smile Certificate of Authenticity	3¼ x 7⅜

MANUFACTURER/MARKING
Simon & Schuster, Inc., licensed by United Media, Enesco Corp. 045544679787 677752

ITEM	SIZE
Advertisement - Happy 100th Birthday! Schedule of Events	8½ x 11

MANUFACTURER/MARKING

ITEM	SIZE
Advertisement - Happy 2016 from Tom and Joni's collection to yours!	1⅝ x 2½

MANUFACTURER/MARKING
Blessings and Raggedy Love…Peace

ITEM	SIZE
Advertisement - Happy is a Heart Full of Friendship Certificate of Authenticity	3¼ x 7⅜

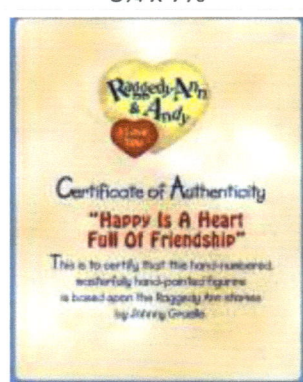

MANUFACTURER/MARKING
Simon & Schuster, Inc., licensed by United Media, Enesco Corp. 045544468688 823546

ITEM	SIZE
Advertisement - Harvest Friendship, Gather Love Certificate of Authenticity	3¼ x 7⅜

MANUFACTURER/MARKING
Simon & Schuster, Inc., licensed by United Media, Enesco Corp. 045544272759 104397

ITEM	SIZE
Advertisement - Have a Happy, Jolly Time Certificate of Authenticity	3¼ x 7⅜

MANUFACTURER/MARKING
1999 Simon & Schuster, Inc., Enesco Corp. 597457 93RA540

ITEM	SIZE
Advertisement - Have a Heart Certificate of Authenticity	3¼ x 7⅜

MANUFACTURER/MARKING
Simon & Schuster, Inc., Enesco Corp. 045544652537 642088

ITEM	SIZE
Advertisement - He Loves Me Certificate of Authenticity	3¼ x 7⅜

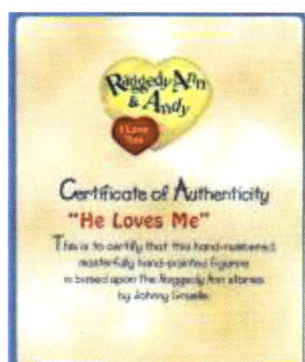

MANUFACTURER/MARKING
Simon & Schuster, Inc., Enesco Corp. 045544649063 640476

ITEM	SIZE
Advertisement - Heartfelt Hugs Make Happy Friends Certificate of Authenticity	3¼ x 7⅜

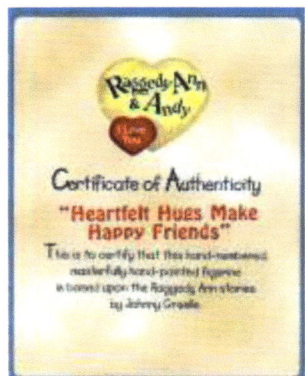

MANUFACTURER/MARKING
Simon & Schuster, Inc., Enesco Corp. 045544649087 640492

ITEM	SIZE
Advertisement - Hello Sunshine Certificate of Authenticity	3¼ x 7⅜

MANUFACTURER/MARKING
Simon & Schuster, Inc., licensed by United Media, Enesco Corp. 06222 045544550444

ITEM	SIZE
Advertisement - Here's a peek at the four new Raggedy Ann and Andy sculptures from The Danbury Mint	8½ x 11

MANUFACTURER/MARKING
1999 Simon & Schuster, Inc., The Danbury Mint, AAF/2L

ITEM	SIZE
Advertisement - Hobby Center Toys	4⅝ x 4¾

MANUFACTURER/MARKING

Raggedy Ann, the original doll with a heart will become a Christmas tradition

ITEM	SIZE
Advertisement - Holidays Go Hand in Hand with your Discover Card and Target Guest Card	3 x 7

MANUFACTURER/MARKING

Snowden 1998 Dayton Hudson Corp., Raggedy Ann and Andy 1998 Simon & Schuster, Inc.

ITEM	SIZE
Advertisement - Home Cookin' Certificate of Authenticity	3¾ x 6¾

MANUFACTURER/MARKING

2000 Simon & Schuster, Inc., The Danbury Mint A807, Peter B. Maglathlin, Director

ITEM	SIZE
Advertisement - Hop Over Troubles with a Happy Heart Inside Certificate of Authenticity	3¼ x 7⅜

MANUFACTURER/MARKING

Simon & Schuster, Inc., licensed by United Media, Enesco Corp. 045544679763 677736

ITEM	SIZE
Advertisement - How Nice to Have Such a Happy Sunny Friend Certificate of Authenticity	3¼ x 7⅜

MANUFACTURER/MARKING
Simon & Schuster, Inc., licensed by United Media, Enesco Corp. 045544679770 677744

ITEM	SIZE
Advertisement - I ♥ You Certificate of Authenticity	3¼ x 7⅜

MANUFACTURER/MARKING
Simon & Schuster, Inc., licensed by United Media, Enesco Corp. 045544643108 783684

ITEM	SIZE
Advertisement - I Found My Hero in You Certificate of Authenticity	3¼ x 7⅜

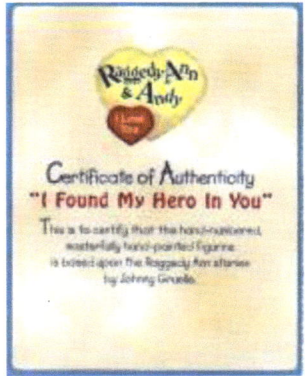

MANUFACTURER/MARKING
Simon & Schuster, Inc., licensed by United Media, Enesco Corp. 045544392563 290874

ITEM	SIZE
Advertisement - I hope they'll like us...and let us stay, Raggedy Ann and Raggedy Andy sitting in a wagon next to a stack of blocks	10⅜ x 12¾

MANUFACTURER/MARKING
Globe-Democrat Sunday Magazine, December 22, 1957

ITEM	SIZE
Advertisement - I Love Every Blooming Thing About You Certificate of Authenticity	3¼ x 7⅜

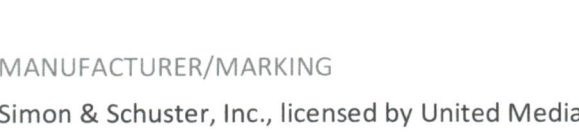

MANUFACTURER/MARKING
Simon & Schuster, Inc., licensed by United Media, Enesco Corp. 106219 045544550413

ITEM	SIZE
Advertisement - I Love You Certificate of Authenticity	3¼ x 7⅜

MANUFACTURER/MARKING
Simon & Schuster, Inc., Enesco Corp. 045544652520 642061

ITEM	SIZE
Advertisement - I Walk on Air with a Friend Like You Certificate of Authenticity	3¼ x 7⅜

MANUFACTURER/MARKING
Simon & Schuster, Inc., licensed by United Media, Enesco Corp. 045544643092 783676

ITEM	SIZE
Advertisement - Ice Capades, Madison Square Garden	4¼ x 6⅞

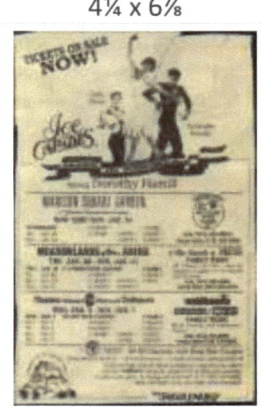

MANUFACTURER/MARKING
Starring Dorothy Hamill, Presented by Leggs Sheer Energy Panty Hose

ITEM	SIZE
Advertisement - Ice Capades, Nassau Coliseum	4 x 6

MANUFACTURER/MARKING

Starring Dorothy Hammill, Presented by Leggs Sheer Energy Panty Hose

ITEM	SIZE
Advertisement - Ideal Collector's Raggedy Ann and Andy Porcelain Dolls Certificate of Quality	5¾ x 9

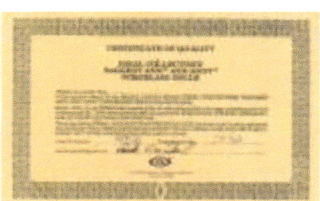

MANUFACTURER/MARKING

1983 Ideal 1,332

ITEM	SIZE
Advertisement - If Friends Were Flowers, I'd Pick You Certificate of Authenticity	3¼ x 7⅜

MANUFACTURER/MARKING

Simon & Schuster, Inc., Enesco Corp. 04554460428494, 544914

ITEM	SIZE
Advertisement - If These Walls Could Talk, Arcola, IL Mural Tour	3¾ x 8½

MANUFACTURER/MARKING

ITEM	SIZE
Advertisement - Image Checks, Raggedy Ann and Andy make their check debut	8½ x 11

MANUFACTURER/MARKING
Image Checks, Little Rock, AR

ITEM	SIZE
Advertisement - In Loving Memory of Tom Wannamaker	5½ x 8½

MANUFACTURER/MARKING
Born March 8, 1943, At Rest March 29, 2016

ITEM	SIZE
Advertisement - It's Always Best to Give from the Heart Certificate of Authenticity	3¼ x 7⅜

MANUFACTURER/MARKING
Simon & Schuster, Inc., licensed by United Media, Enesco Corp. 045544711883 709093

ITEM	SIZE
Advertisement - It's Great to be Alive When You're Five Certificate of Authenticity	3¼ x 7⅜

MANUFACTURER/MARKING
Simon & Schuster, Inc., licensed by United Media, Enesco Corp. 045544151672 823740

ITEM	SIZE
Advertisement - It's So Dandy You're So Handy Certificate of Authenticity	3¼ x 7⅜

MANUFACTURER/MARKING
Simon & Schuster, Inc., licensed by United Media, Enesco Corp. 045544392792 291005

ITEM	SIZE
Advertisement - It's Time for the Raggedy Ann Festival! Coloring Contest, Tea Party	8½ x 11

MANUFACTURER/MARKING
Call 234-6841

ITEM	SIZE
Advertisement - J.C. Penney Musical Dolls	8⅛ x 11

MANUFACTURER/MARKING
1970 Penney

ITEM	SIZE
Advertisement - J.C. Penney Novelty Tees	7¼ x 7⅞

MANUFACTURER/MARKING

ITEM	SIZE
Advertisement - Japanese Merchandise for 1993-1994, Bags and Pouches	8½ x 11½

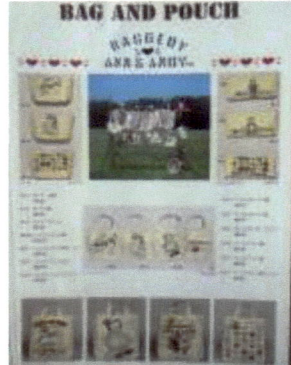

MANUFACTURER/MARKING

1994 Macmillan, Inc.

ITEM	SIZE
Advertisement - Japanese Merchandise for 1993-1994, Baskets, buckets, door stops, picture frames	8½ x 11½

MANUFACTURER/MARKING

1993 Macmillan, Inc., Phoenix Corporation

ITEM	SIZE
Advertisement - Japanese Merchandise for 1993-1994, Blankets, Pillows, Rugs, Towels, Washcloths	8½ x 11½

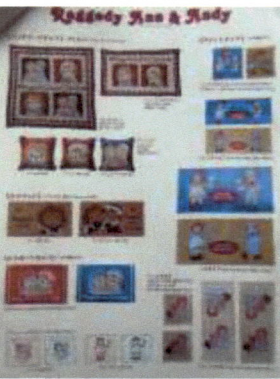

MANUFACTURER/MARKING

© & ™ Simon & Schuster, Inc., licensed by United Media

ITEM	SIZE
Advertisement - Japanese Merchandise for 1993-1994, Bowls, Creamer, Dishes, Salt and Pepper Shakers	8½ x 11½

MANUFACTURER/MARKING

1993 Macmillan, Inc., Kiri China Industry Co., Ltd.

ITEM	SIZE
Advertisement - Japanese Merchandise for 1993-1994, Bowls, Cups and Dishes	8½ x 11½

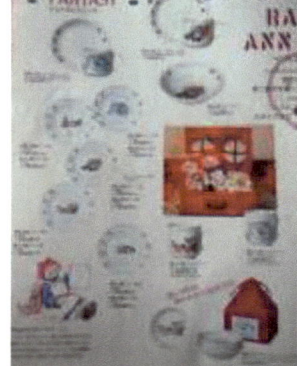

MANUFACTURER/MARKING

ITEM	SIZE
Advertisement - Japanese Merchandise for 1993-1994, Buckets, Cans, Cups, Dolls, Jewelry Boxes, Key Rings	8½ x 11½

MANUFACTURER/MARKING

Young Epoch Co.

ITEM	SIZE
Advertisement - Japanese Merchandise for 1993-1994, Clothing Hangers, Desk Accessories, Picture Frames	8½ x 11½

MANUFACTURER/MARKING

1994 Macmillan, Inc.

ITEM	SIZE
Advertisement - Japanese Merchandise for 1993-1994, Coffee Canisters, Coffee Pots, Cups, Dishes	8½ x 11½

MANUFACTURER/MARKING

1993 Macmillan, Inc., Kusunoki Toy Co.

ITEM

Advertisement - Japanese Merchandise for 1993-1994, Creamer, Cups, Dishes, Glasses, Rubber Stamps, Sugar Bowl, Teapot, Toothbrush Holder

SIZE

8½ x 11½

MANUFACTURER/MARKING

Axcis, Inc.

ITEM

Advertisement - Japanese Merchandise for 1993-1994, Cups, Teabag Holders, Trinket Boxes, Trinket Holders

SIZE

8½ x 11½

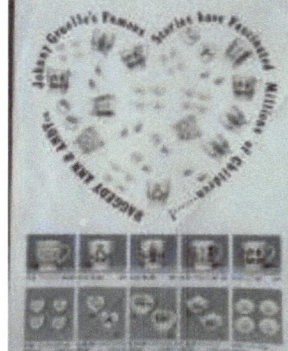

MANUFACTURER/MARKING

ITEM

Advertisement - Japanese Merchandise for 1993-1994, Dolls and Key Rings

SIZE

8½ x 11½

MANUFACTURER/MARKING

Young Epoch Co., Ltd.

ITEM

Advertisement - Japanese Merchandise for 1993-1994, Glasses and Jars

SIZE

8½ x 11½

MANUFACTURER/MARKING

1994 Macmillan, Inc.

ITEM

Advertisement - Japanese Merchandise for 1993-1994, Key Rings, Mirrors, Necklaces, Pins, Plaques, Ponytail Holders

SIZE

8½ x 11½

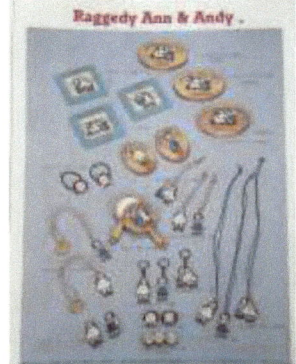

MANUFACTURER/MARKING

1993 Macmillan, Inc., Phoenix Corporation

ITEM

Advertisement - Japanese Merchandise for 1993-1994, Magnets

SIZE

8½ x 11½

MANUFACTURER/MARKING

1994 Macmillan, Inc.

ITEM

Advertisement - Japanese Merchandise for 1993-1994, Placemats and Rugs

SIZE

8½ x 11½

MANUFACTURER/MARKING

1994 Macmillan, Inc.

ITEM

Advertisement - Japanese Merchandise for 1993-1994, Postcards

SIZE

8½ x 11½

MANUFACTURER/MARKING

ITEM	SIZE
Advertisement - Japanese Merchandise for 2000, Decals, Notebooks, Portfolios, Quilts, Stationery, Towel Wraps, Umbrellas	17 x 11⅝

MANUFACTURER/MARKING

©Simon & Schuster, Inc., Licensed by United Media, BEP Communications Group K.K.

ITEM	SIZE
Advertisement - Japanese Merchandise for 2002, Calendars, Calendar Covers, Make-up Case, Notebooks, Seals, Transfers	17 x 11⅝

MANUFACTURER/MARKING

©Simon & Schuster, Inc., Licensed by United Media, BEP Communications Group K.K.

ITEM	SIZE
Advertisement - Japanese Merchandise for 2004, Calendars, Calendar Cover, Cans, Drawer, Towels, Washcloths	17 x 11⅝

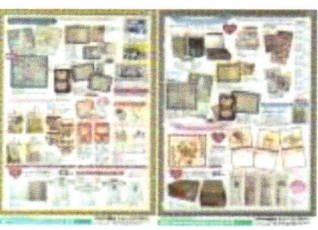

MANUFACTURER/MARKING

©Simon & Schuster, Inc., Licensed by United Media, BEP Communications Group K.K.

ITEM	SIZE
Advertisement - Japanese Merchandise for 2005, Address Book, Address Book Covers, Calendars, Drink Bottles, Mouse Pad, Name Tags, Pen, Pencil, Rugs	17 x 11⅝

MANUFACTURER/MARKING

©Simon & Schuster, Inc., Licensed by United Media, BEP Communications Group K.K.

ITEM	SIZE
Advertisement - Japanese Merchandise for 2006, Bags, Calendars, Calendar Covers, Coasters, Make-up Case, Notebooks, Plastic Bag Holders, Trays	17 x 11⅝

MANUFACTURER/MARKING	
©Simon & Schuster, Inc., Licensed by United Media, BEP Communications Group K.K.	

ITEM	SIZE
Advertisement - Japanese Merchandise for 2012-2013, Bags, Bottles, Calendars, Calendar Covers, Chopsticks, Fabric, Notebooks, Post Cards, Umbrellas, Watches	17 x 11⅝

MANUFACTURER/MARKING	
©Simon & Schuster, Inc., Licensed by United Media, BEP Communications Group K.K.	

ITEM	SIZE
Advertisement - Japanese Merchandise, Address Book, Address Book Cover, Books, Cans, Drawer, Notebooks, Recipe Cards, Stationery, Tape, Tray	17 x 11⅝

MANUFACTURER/MARKING	
©Simon & Schuster, Inc., Licensed by United Media, BEP Communications Group K.K.	

ITEM	SIZE
Advertisement - Japanese Merchandise, Address Book, Bags, Coloring Books, Decals, Drink Bottles with Holders, Lace, Notebooks, Pencil Case, Stationery, Wrapping Paper	17 x 11⅝

MANUFACTURER/MARKING	
©Simon & Schuster, Inc., Licensed by United Media, BEP Communications Group K.K.	

ITEM

Advertisement - Japanese Merchandise, Address Books, Address Book Covers, Calendars, Calendar Frames, Name Tags, Pen, Pencil, Pillows

SIZE

8½ x 11½

MANUFACTURER/MARKING

©Simon & Schuster, Inc., Licensed by United Media, BEP Communications Group K.K.

ITEM

Advertisement - Japanese Merchandise, Bags, Boxes, Drink Bottles, Erasers, Notebooks, Pencils, Pen, Pencil Cases, Rugs, Stationery, Towel Wraps, Umbrellas

SIZE

17 x 11⅝

MANUFACTURER/MARKING

©Simon & Schuster, Inc., Licensed by United Media, BEP Communications Group K.K.

ITEM

Advertisement - Japanese Merchandise, Bags, Coasters, Drawer, Make-up Case, Towel Wraps, Tray, Umbrellas. Washcloths

SIZE

17 x 11⅝

MANUFACTURER/MARKING

©Simon & Schuster, Inc., Licensed by United Media, BEP Communications Group K.K.

ITEM

Advertisement - Japanese Merchandise, Bags, Decals, Drawer, Notebooks, Pencils, Umbrellas, Washcloths

SIZE

17 x 11⅝

MANUFACTURER/MARKING

©Simon & Schuster, Inc., Licensed by United Media, BEP Communications Group K.K.

ITEM

Advertisement - Japanese Merchandise, Bowls, Cups, Dishes, Notebooks, Pencil Cases, Rugs, Stationery

SIZE

8½ x 11½

MANUFACTURER/MARKING

©Simon & Schuster, Inc., Licensed by United Media, BEP Communications Group K.K.

ITEM

Advertisement - Japanese Merchandise, Calendar, Calendar Frames, Drawer, Drink Bottles, Notebooks, Pen, Pencils, Pencil Cases, Portfolios

SIZE

17 x 11⅝

MANUFACTURER/MARKING

©Simon & Schuster, Inc., Licensed by United Media, BEP Communications Group K.K.

ITEM

Advertisement - Japanese Merchandise, Calendars, Calendar Cover, Decal, Notebooks, Rugs, Seals, Stationery, Tape, Washcloths

SIZE

17 x 11⅝

MANUFACTURER/MARKING

©Simon & Schuster, Inc., Licensed by United Media, BEP Communications Group K.K.

ITEM

Advertisement - Japanese Merchandise, Calendars, Calendar Cover, Mouse Pad, Notebooks, Pencil Case, Recipe Cards, Recipe Card Boxes, Stationery

SIZE

17 x 11⅝

MANUFACTURER/MARKING

©Simon & Schuster, Inc., Licensed by United Media, BEP Communications Group K.K.

ITEM

Advertisement - Japanese Merchandise, Calendars, Calendar Covers, Cans, Decals, Notebooks, Stationery, Tape, Tea, Towels, Washcloths

SIZE

17 x 11⅝

MANUFACTURER/MARKING

©Simon & Schuster, Inc., Licensed by United Media, BEP Communications Group K.K.

ITEM

Advertisement - Japanese Merchandise, Calendars, Cans, Erasers, Notebook, Note Paper, Pen, Pencils, Pencil Cases, Rulers,

SIZE

17 x 11⅝

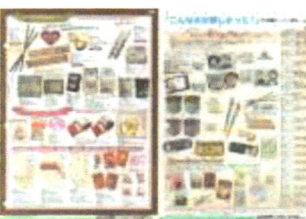

MANUFACTURER/MARKING

©Simon & Schuster, Inc., Licensed by United Media, BEP Communications Group K.K.

ITEM

Advertisement - Japanese Merchandise, Coloring Books, Cups, Dishes, Jars, Mouse Pad, Notebooks, Pitchers, Rugs, Slippers, Tissue Box Holders, Toilet Tissue Holders

SIZE

8½ x 11½

MANUFACTURER/MARKING

©Simon & Schuster, Inc., Licensed by United Media, BEP Communications Group K.K.

ITEM

Advertisement - Japanese Merchandise, Drawer, Notebooks, Pen, Pencil, Pillows, Sewing Boxes, Umbrellas, Washcloths

SIZE

17 x 11⅝

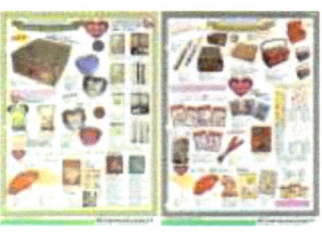

MANUFACTURER/MARKING

©Simon & Schuster, Inc., Licensed by United Media, BEP Communications Group K.K.

ITEM

Advertisement - Japanese Merchandise, Napkins, Notebooks, Pen, Pencil, Pencil Case, Stationery

SIZE

17 x 11⅝

MANUFACTURER/MARKING

©Simon & Schuster, Inc., Licensed by United Media, BEP Communications Group K.K.

ITEM

Advertisement - Japanese Merchandise, Paper Ephemera, Pillows, Umbrellas, Writing Instruments

SIZE

17 x 11⅝

MANUFACTURER/MARKING

©Simon & Schuster, Inc., Licensed by United Media, BEP Communications Group K.K.

ITEM

Advertisement - Japanese Merchandise, Pillows, Pillowcase, Quilt, Rugs, Toilet Covers, Toilet Mats, Towels, Washcloths

SIZE

17 x 11⅝

MANUFACTURER/MARKING

©Simon & Schuster, Inc., Licensed by United Media, BEP Communications Group K.K.

ITEM

Advertisement - Japanese Merchandise, Towels and Washcloths

SIZE

8½ x 11½

MANUFACTURER/MARKING

©Simon & Schuster, Inc., Licensed by United Media, BEP Communications Group K.K.

ITEM	SIZE
Advertisement - Japanese Merchandise, T-shirts	8½ x 11½

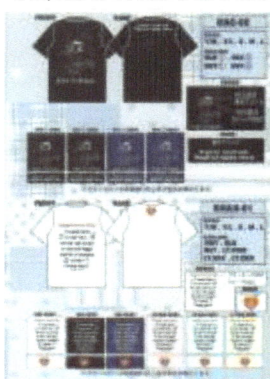

MANUFACTURER/MARKING
©Simon & Schuster, Inc., Licensed by United Media, BEP Communications Group K.K.

ITEM	SIZE
Advertisement - Japanese Merchandise, T-shirts	17 x 11⅝

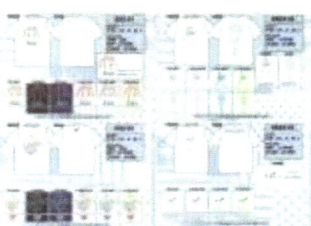

MANUFACTURER/MARKING
©Simon & Schuster, Inc., Licensed by United Media, BEP Communications Group K.K.

ITEM	SIZE
Advertisement - Jenn Air	7⅝ x 10½

MANUFACTURER/MARKING
Remember the days when cooking for a crowd wasn't a chore?

ITEM	SIZE
Advertisement - Johnny Gruelle's Marcella and Raggedy Ann by Haut Melton, A special set to warm your heart and make you smile	3⅝ x 8½

MANUFACTURER/MARKING
R. John Wright Dolls, Inc., Bennington, VT, Simon & Schuster, Inc., licensed by United Media

ITEM

Advertisement - Johnny Gruelle's Marcella, A Raggedy Ann All Felt Doll Story

SIZE

2¾ x 4¼

MANUFACTURER/MARKING

R. John Wright Dolls, Inc., Bennington, VT, Simon & Schuster, Inc., licensed by United Media

ITEM

Advertisement - Johnny Gruelle's Marcella, A Raggedy Ann Story by Haut Melton

SIZE

8½ x 11

MANUFACTURER/MARKING

R. John Wright Dolls, Inc., Bennington, VT, Simon & Schuster, Inc., licensed by United Media

ITEM

Advertisement - Johnny Gruelle's New Johnny Mouse Doll for Woman's World Girls and Boys

SIZE

5¼ x 7⅜

MANUFACTURER/MARKING

75¢ prepaid Woman's World, 107 South Clinton Street, Chicago

ITEM

Advertisement - Johnny Mouse Picnic Tea Party 2005

SIZE

5½ x 8½

MANUFACTURER/MARKING

Simon & Schuster, Inc., licensed by United Media, Joni Gruelle 2005

ITEM

Advertisement - Johnny Mouse Picnic Tea Party Entrance Ticket

SIZE

2 x 5½

MANUFACTURER/MARKING

Saturday, May 21, 2005, 10:30 a.m.

ITEM

Advertisement - Join the Johnny Gruelle Raggedy Ann and Andy Museum

SIZE

8½ x 11

MANUFACTURER/MARKING

For the Heart's Sake!

ITEM

Advertisement - Joy and Love are Truly Catching Certificate of Authenticity

SIZE

3¼ x 7⅜

MANUFACTURER/MARKING

Simon & Schuster, Inc., licensed by United Media, Enesco Corp. 045544679831 677809

ITEM

Advertisement - Jump Into Each New Day Certificate of Authenticity

SIZE

3¼ x 7⅜

MANUFACTURER/MARKING

Simon & Schuster, Inc., licensed by United Media, Enesco Corp. 106221 045544550437

ITEM

Advertisement - Just for You Certificate of Authenticity

SIZE

3⅜ x 6⅜

MANUFACTURER/MARKING

Simon & Schuster, Inc., A807 TM

ITEM

Advertisement - Keeper of the Dolls Certificate of Authenticity

SIZE

3½ x 5½

MANUFACTURER/MARKING

Sharon A. Billings

ITEM

Advertisement - Keystone Camera Company

SIZE

10⅝ x 13⅝

MANUFACTURER/MARKING

February 23, 1957 Saturday Evening Post

ITEM

Advertisement - Kind Hearts are the Garden, Kind Thoughts are the Root, Kind Words are the Blossom, Kind Deeds are the Fruit Certificate of Authenticity

SIZE

3¼ x 7⅜

MANUFACTURER/MARKING

Simon & Schuster, Inc., licensed by United Media, Enesco Corp. 106215 045544549868

ITEM

Advertisement - L.A.F. Venture Celebrating the Arcola Festival

SIZE

8½ x 11

MANUFACTURER/MARKING

L.A.F. Venture, Inc., June 30, 2002, Celebrating the Arcola Festival

ITEM

Advertisement - Leap Frog Certificate of Authenticity

SIZE

3¾ x 6¾

MANUFACTURER/MARKING

The Danbury Mint, Peter B. Maglathlin, Director A807

ITEM

Advertisement - Lending a Hand Makes the Job Twice as Fun Certificate of Authenticity

SIZE

3¼ x 7⅜

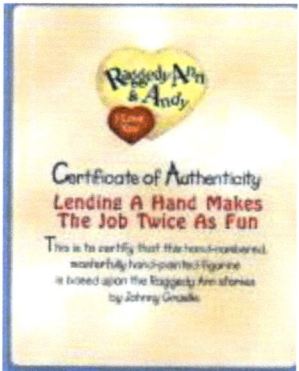

MANUFACTURER/MARKING

Simon & Schuster, Inc., licensed by United Media, Enesco Corp. 045544760379 953172 2392

ITEM

Advertisement - Let Your Heart Bloom Certificate of Authenticity

SIZE

3¼ x 7⅜

MANUFACTURER/MARKING

Simon & Schuster, Inc., licensed by United Media, Enesco Corp. 106220 045544550420

ITEM	SIZE
Advertisement - Life in America: Raggedy Ann Dolls	4⅜ x 6⅛

MANUFACTURER/MARKING

© Grolier, Inc. 1997, 68-10

ITEM	SIZE
Advertisement - Life is What You Make It Certificate of Authenticity	3¼ x 7⅜

MANUFACTURER/MARKING

Simon & Schuster, Inc., licensed by United Media, Enesco Corp. 04444711920 709107

ITEM	SIZE
Advertisement - Life's Lessons are Learned Every Day Certificate of Authenticity	3¼ x 7⅜

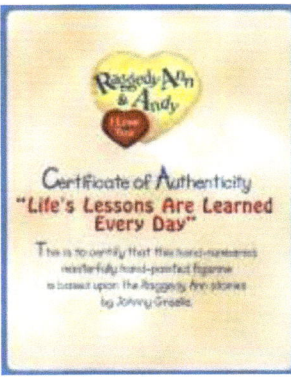

MANUFACTURER/MARKING

Simon & Schuster, Inc., licensed by United Media, Enesco Corp. 045544390514 289914

ITEM	SIZE
Advertisement - Lockerbie Square Tour of Homes and Gardens	8½ x 11

MANUFACTURER/MARKING

Saturday and Sunday, June 13-14, 11 a.m. to 5 p.m.

ITEM

Advertisement - Long Island Floor Covering Dealers

SIZE

4½ x 5

MANUFACTURER/MARKING

Presents Kid- Tough Floors from Congoleum

ITEM

Advertisement - Look on the Bright Side of Life Certificate of Authenticity

SIZE

3¼ x 7⅜

MANUFACTURER/MARKING

Simon & Schuster, Inc., licensed by United Media, Enesco Corp. 045544711883 709069

ITEM

Advertisement - Look Your Best to Feel Your Best Certificate of Authenticity

SIZE

3¼ x 7⅜

MANUFACTURER/MARKING

Simon & Schuster, Inc., licensed by United Media, Enesco Corp. 045544760896 953121

ITEM

Advertisement - Love is Blind by Bessie Pease Gutmann

SIZE

7⅝ x 10½

MANUFACTURER/MARKING

Bessie Pease Gutmann is a trademark of the Balliol Corp., © 1989 HC, Macmillan, Inc.

ITEM	SIZE
Advertisement - Magic Pen Painting Books	8½ x 11

MANUFACTURER/MARKING

© Macmillan, Inc.

ITEM	SIZE
Advertisement - Magical Hearts Exhibit	8½ x 11

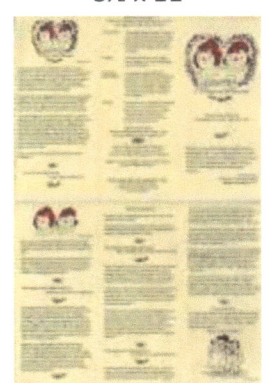

MANUFACTURER/MARKING

November 23, 1990 to May 16, 1991, Indiana State Museum

ITEM	SIZE
Advertisement - Magical Hour Bed Registration Card	3⅝ x 5¼

MANUFACTURER/MARKING

#161/250 R. John Wright Dolls, Inc., Bennington, VT, Simon & Schuster, Inc., licensed by United Media

ITEM	SIZE
Advertisement - Marcella and Her Raggedy Family	8½ x 11

MANUFACTURER/MARKING

The Lawton Doll Company, 1988 Collection

ITEM

Advertisement - Marcella and Her Raggedy Family Certificate of Authenticity

SIZE

4 x 5¼

MANUFACTURER/MARKING

Childhood Classics Collection, 1998 Wendy Lawton, 1997 Simon & Schuster, #591/1000

ITEM

Advertisement - Marcella and Raggedy Ann and Andy by Madame Alexander Certificate of Authenticity

SIZE

4¾ x 7⅝

MANUFACTURER/MARKING

#446/500, 2008 Madame Alexander Doll Co., Simon & Schuster, Inc. #46390, licensed by United Media

ITEM

Advertisement - Marcella and Raggedy Ann by Haut Melton Certificate of Authenticity

SIZE

5½ x 8½

MANUFACTURER/MARKING

Martha Haut Melton and Kent Melton #32 of 1,000

ITEM

Advertisement - Marcella and Raggedy Ann by R. John Wright Certificate of Authenticity

SIZE

3⅝ x 5⅜

MANUFACTURER/MARKING

#164/250 R. John Wright Dolls, Inc., Bennington, VT, Simon & Schuster, Inc., licensed by United Media, Year of Issue: 2005

ITEM	**SIZE**
Advertisement - Marcella and Raggedy Ann by R. John Wright Registration Card	3⅝ x 5⅜

MANUFACTURER/MARKING

#164/250 R. John Wright Dolls, Inc., Bennington, VT, Simon & Schuster, Inc., licensed by United Media, Year of Issue: 2005

ITEM	**SIZE**
Advertisement - Marcella and Raggedy Ann by Wendy Lawton	7½ x 9¾

MANUFACTURER/MARKING

1988 Macmillan, Inc., Lawtons, 2516 Lander Avenue, Turlock, CA 95380

ITEM	**SIZE**
Advertisement - Marcella and Raggedy Ann by Wendy Lawton Certificate of Authenticity	4 x 6

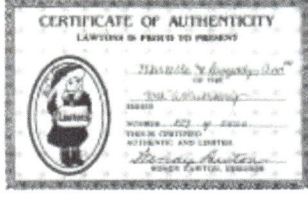

MANUFACTURER/MARKING

Wendy Lawton Designer, 229 of 2,500

ITEM	**SIZE**
Advertisement - Marcella and Raggedy Ann, Miniature Forever Friends and Raggedy Ann's Bed	8½ x 11

MANUFACTURER/MARKING

R. John Wright Dolls, Inc., Bennington, VT, Simon & Schuster, Inc., licensed by United Media

ITEM	SIZE
Advertisement - Marcella Doll with Raggedy Ann Official Collector Registration Card	4 x 5½

MANUFACTURER/MARKING

No. A1502639MA, 2002 Madame Alexander Doll Co., Inc.

ITEM	SIZE
Advertisement - Marcella Loves Raggedy Ann 95th Birthday Official Collector Registration Card	⅛ x 5½

MANUFACTURER/MARKING

2002 Alexander Doll Co., Inc. A1736687MA

ITEM	SIZE
Advertisement - Marcella Takes a Trip with Raggedy Ann and Andy Official Collector Registration Card	4⅛ x 5½

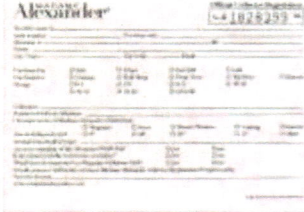

MANUFACTURER/MARKING

2002 Alexander Doll Co., Inc. A1828399MA

ITEM	SIZE
Advertisement - Marcella's Sun Porch Festival Menu	5 x 7

MANUFACTURER/MARKING

5th Annual Raggedy Ann and Andy Festival Menu

ITEM	SIZE
Advertisement - Maxwell House, Everybody knows the sign of good coffee.	10 x 13

MANUFACTURER/MARKING

February 19, 1951 - Life

ITEM	SIZE
Advertisement - McCall's Little Raggedys Patterns	9½ x 14

MANUFACTURER/MARKING

1991 Macmillan, Inc. 5702 and 5418

ITEM	SIZE
Advertisement - McCall's pattern to make 19" Raggedy Ann	3⅜ x 3⅞

MANUFACTURER/MARKING

Pattern to make a 19" doll

ITEM	SIZE
Advertisement - McCall's Patterns	10 x 13

MANUFACTURER/MARKING

1955 McCall's, John B. Gruelle

ITEM	SIZE
Advertisement - McCall's Patterns, Extra! Extra! Raggedy Ann's back in town	10¼ x 13

MANUFACTURER/MARKING

McCall's Pattern Co., 1970 The Bobbs-Merrill Co., Inc.

ITEM	SIZE
Advertisement - Metropolitan Children's Book & Antique Toy Fair	5½ x 8½

MANUFACTURER/MARKING

December 1, 1995-December 2, 1995, Guest Speakers Tasha Tudor and Patricia Hall

ITEM	SIZE
Advertisement - Mid-Ohio Historical Museum, Inc.	3⅝ x 8½

MANUFACTURER/MARKING

ITEM	SIZE
Advertisement - Monarch Electric Cook Book	8½ x 11

MANUFACTURER/MARKING

Monarch Electric Range 1925

ITEM	SIZE
Advertisement - Motorola TV, Give a Motorola and you know you give the best	10⅛ x 13⅝

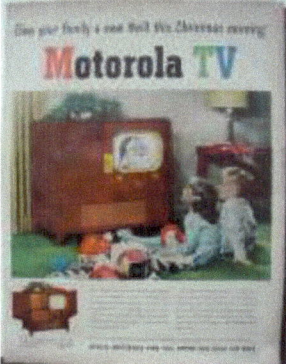

MANUFACTURER/MARKING

12/4/1950 Life

ITEM	SIZE
Advertisement - Mr. Twee Deedle's Tea Party Ticket for afternoon seating	2 x 5¼

MANUFACTURER/MARKING

Saturday, June 10th, 1:30 p.m.

ITEM	SIZE
Advertisement - Music Brings Friends Together Certificate of Authenticity	3¼ x 7⅛

MANUFACTURER/MARKING

Simon & Schuster, Inc., licensed by United Media, Enesco Corp. 04554484626848744

ITEM	SIZE
Advertisement - Music is the Laughter in Our Hearts Certificate of Authenticity	3¼ x 7⅛

MANUFACTURER/MARKING

Simon & Schuster, Inc., licensed by United Media, Enesco Corp. 045544194341 864919

ITEM
Advertisement - Musical hurdy gurdy, talking push-button phone, pencil sharpener, talking alarm clock and power toothbrush

SIZE
8½ x 11

MANUFACTURER/MARKING
1974 Spiegel

ITEM
Advertisement - Musical Raggedy Ann and Andy Bedtime Dolls

SIZE
8⅛ x 11

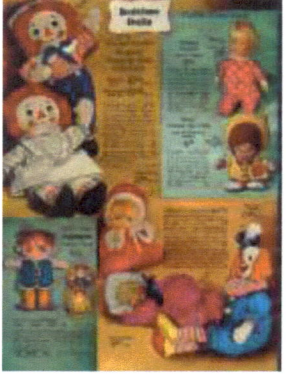

MANUFACTURER/MARKING

ITEM
Advertisement - My Best Friends, Raggedy Ann and Andy

SIZE
11 x 17⅛

MANUFACTURER/MARKING
Simon & Schuster, Inc., licensed by United Media, Susan Wakeen, WRA/bro

ITEM
Advertisement - My Best Friends, Raggedy Ann and Andy Certificate of Authenticity

SIZE
4½ x 6½

MANUFACTURER/MARKING
Susan Wakeen, Artist, Peter B. Maglathlin, Director, The Danbury Mint A2023

ITEM	SIZE
Advertisement - My Best Friends, Raggedy Ann and Andy Posing Instructions	5½ x 8½

MANUFACTURER/MARKING
WRA/1/UPC ©MBI

ITEM	SIZE
Advertisement - My Best Friends, Raggedy Ann and Andy Reservation Application	5½ x 8½

MANUFACTURER/MARKING
Simon & Schuster, Inc., licensed by United Media, Susan Wakeen, WRA/OC

ITEM	SIZE
Advertisement - My Heart's Creations	8½ x 11

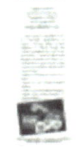 

MANUFACTURER/MARKING
2000 Simon & Schuster, Inc., Licensed by United Media, Megan Keating, Official Licensee

ITEM	SIZE
Advertisement - Nabisco Team Flakes	10 x 13

MANUFACTURER/MARKING
April 29, 1966 - Life

ITEM	SIZE
Advertisement - Not Your Typical Hollywood Couple, But Soon They'll Be Movie Stars	7⅞ x 10⅝

MANUFACTURER/MARKING

1976 The Bobbs-Merrill Co., Inc., International Telephone & Telegraph Corp.

ITEM	SIZE
Advertisement - Nothing's Nicer Than a Sharing Heart Certificate of Authenticity	3¼ x 7⅜

MANUFACTURER/MARKING

Simon & Schuster, Inc., licensed by United Media, Enesco Corp. 045544679824 677795

ITEM	SIZE
Advertisement - One, Two, Three, Come Play With Me Certificate of Authenticity	3¼ x 7⅜

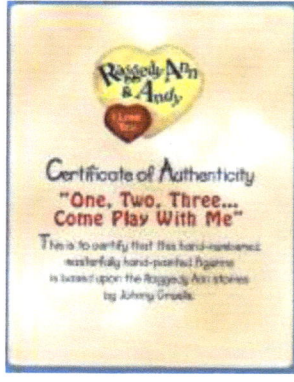

MANUFACTURER/MARKING

Simon & Schuster, Inc., licensed by United Media, Enesco Corp. 045544470759 864889

ITEM	SIZE
Advertisement - Oneida 4 Piece Children's Dish Set, plastic	5¼ x 8¼

MANUFACTURER/MARKING

1977 Carol Wright Gifts, Oneida, Melmac

ITEM	SIZE
Advertisement - Our Friendship has a Special Beat Certificate of Authenticity	3¼ x 7⅛

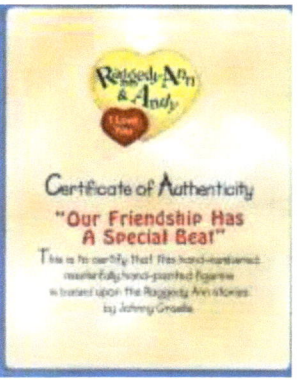

MANUFACTURER/MARKING
Simon & Schuster, Inc., licensed by United Media, Enesco Corp. 044470827 864927

ITEM	SIZE
Advertisement - Our Friendship is Filled with Magic Certificate of Authenticity	3¼ x 7⅜

MANUFACTURER/MARKING
Simon & Schuster, Inc., licensed by United Media, Enesco Corp. 045544272742 104395

ITEM	SIZE
Advertisement - Our Friendship is on a Roll Certificate of Authenticity	3¼ x 7⅜

MANUFACTURER/MARKING
Simon & Schuster, Inc., licensed by United Media, Enesco Corp. 045544470766 864897

ITEM	SIZE
Advertisement - Our Friendship Leads to Happy Trails Certificate of Authenticity	3¼ x 7⅜

MANUFACTURER/MARKING
Simon & Schuster, Inc., licensed by United Media, Enesco Corp. 045544347617 864862

ITEM	SIZE
Advertisement - Participation in the 1996 Raggedy Ann & Andy Festival Parade	8½ x 11

MANUFACTURER/MARKING	
The 7th Annual Festival, Doris Knaus, Annette Ferguson, Brian and I won $10 for third place in Raggedy Ann and Andy Look-A-Like Contest	

ITEM	SIZE
Advertisement - Participation in the 1998 Raggedy Ann & Andy Festival Parade	8½ x 11

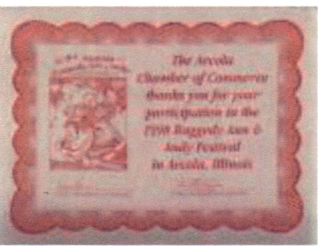

MANUFACTURER/MARKING	
The 9th Annual Festival, Doris Knaus, Annette Ferguson	

ITEM	SIZE
Advertisement - Peek A Boo, I Love You Certificate of Authenticity	3⅛ x 7½

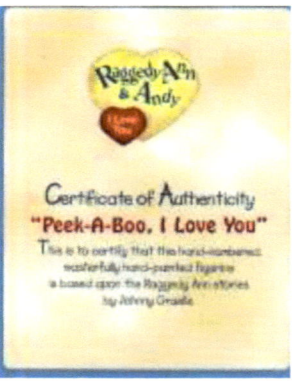

MANUFACTURER/MARKING	
Simon & Schuster, Inc., licensed by United Media, Enesco Corp. 045544642873 783560	

ITEM	SIZE
Advertisement - Picnic Fun Certificate of Authenticity	3¾ x 6¾

MANUFACTURER/MARKING	
Simon & Schuster, Inc., A807, Peter B. Maglathlin, Director	

ITEM	SIZE
Advertisement - Pipka Raggedy Ann and Andy Santa Certificate of Authenticity	3 x 4

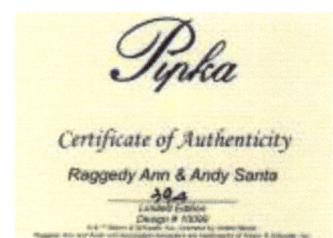

MANUFACTURER/MARKING

Pipka #394, Design Number 10099, Simon & Schuster, Inc., licensed by United Media

ITEM	SIZE
Advertisement - Pitty Pat Miniatures, Inc.	8½ x 11

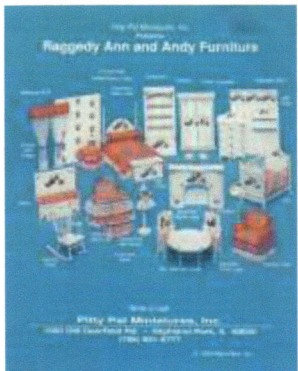

MANUFACTURER/MARKING

1990 Macmillan, Inc., Pitty Pat Miniatures, Inc.

ITEM	SIZE
Advertisement - Playdate with Raggedy Ann Doll Official Collector Registration Card	4 x 5½

MANUFACTURER/MARKING

No. L0810429MA, 2002 Madame Alexander Doll Co., Inc.

ITEM	SIZE
Advertisement - Playful Rag Dolls quilts	8½ x 11

MANUFACTURER/MARKING

1974 Spiegel

ITEM	SIZE
Advertisement - Playtex Dryper	8⅜ x 10⅞

MANUFACTURER/MARKING

International Latex Corp., Playtex Park, Dover, Delaware 1951

ITEM	SIZE
Advertisement - Post Toasties Double-Thick Corn Flakes	10⅜ x 13⅝

MANUFACTURER/MARKING

February 1926, P.C. Co.

ITEM	SIZE
Advertisement - Precision Watch Co., Inc.	8½ x 11

MANUFACTURER/MARKING

Children's Digitals with Skippy, Moppet and Jack and Jill Characters, 1973 Precision Watch Co.

ITEM	SIZE
Advertisement - Premiere Edition Raggedy Andy by R. John Wright Dolls, Inc. Certificate of Authenticity	3⅝ x 5⅜

MANUFACTURER/MARKING

#0550/1,000 R. John Wright Dolls, Inc., Bennington, VT, Simon & Schuster, Inc., licensed by United Media, Year of Issue: 20004

ITEM

Advertisement - Premiere Edition Raggedy Ann by R. John Wright Dolls, Inc. Certificate of Authenticity

SIZE

3⅜ x 5⅜

MANUFACTURER/MARKING

#0550/1,000 R. John Wright Dolls, Inc., Bennington, VT, Simon & Schuster, Inc., licensed by United Media, Year of Issue: 2004

ITEM

Advertisement - Proceeds from the sale of the limited edition nutcrackers

SIZE

3 x 7⅜

MANUFACTURER/MARKING

$250 plus shipping

ITEM

Advertisement - Programs and Events at Strong National Museum of Play

SIZE

5½ x 8½

MANUFACTURER/MARKING

Summer 2010

ITEM

Advertisement - Pure Pak, Your Personal Milk Container

SIZE

10¼ x 14

MANUFACTURER/MARKING

Open the door to convenience - Pure Pak division, Ex-Cell-O Corp.

ITEM | SIZE
Advertisement - R. John Wright Collections for 2005 | 11¼ x 17⅞

MANUFACTURER/MARKING

ITEM | SIZE
Advertisement - Radio and Battery Powered Toothbrushes | 8⅛ x 11

MANUFACTURER/MARKING

1974 The Bobbs-Merrill Co., Inc., J.C. Penney

ITEM | SIZE
Advertisement - Radio City Music Hall | 6 x 9

MANUFACTURER/MARKING

Week beginning Thursday, December 18, 1975

ITEM | SIZE
Advertisement - Rag-Doll Bookends | 6 x 8

MANUFACTURER/MARKING

Michelle Holzapfel's indulgent $13,500 rag doll Bookends, at Peter Joseph Gallery

ITEM	SIZE
Advertisement - Rag-Doll decoupage and candle craft kit	8½ x 11

MANUFACTURER/MARKING

1974 Spiegel

ITEM	SIZE
Advertisement - Rag-Doll Exercises	13⅜ x 20½

MANUFACTURER/MARKING

by Dorothy Anne Robinson, Beauty Editor, photographs by Michael A. Vaccaro, Raggedy Ann Doll: F.A.O. Schwarz, April 1964 Ladies Home Journal

ITEM	SIZE
Advertisement - Rag-Doll Ornaments, Metropolitan Museum of Art	3 x 6

MANUFACTURER/MARKING

ITEM	SIZE
Advertisement - Rag-Doll Pair music box	8½ x 11

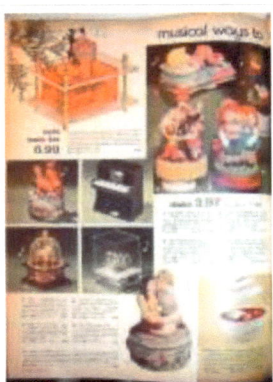

MANUFACTURER/MARKING

1974 Spiegel

ITEM

Advertisement - Raggedy 5K Run, 7th Annual Raggedy Ann Festival

SIZE

8½ x 11

MANUFACTURER/MARKING

April 18, 2009

ITEM

Advertisement - Raggedy Andy Sugar Plum Doll Certificate of Authenticity

SIZE

3⅜ x 6⅛

MANUFACTURER/MARKING

#201 of 5,000

ITEM

Advertisement - Raggedy Ann & Andy...A Patriotic Pair Posing Instructions

SIZE

3½ x 8¼

MANUFACTURER/MARKING

8862/2/UPC, MBI

ITEM

Advertisement - Raggedy Ann & Andy...A Patriotic Pair Reservation Application

SIZE

8½ x 11

MANUFACTURER/MARKING

8862, F636

ITEM	SIZE
Advertisement - Raggedy Ann 100th Birthday Celebration Schedule of Events	8⅝ x 14

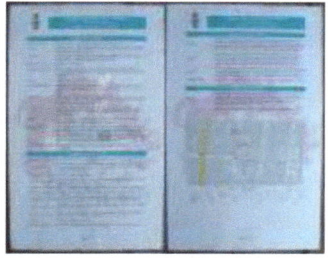

MANUFACTURER/MARKING
Arcola, IL, June 12-14, 2015

ITEM	SIZE
Advertisement - Raggedy Ann and Andy 16" Dolls and 18" Raggedy Ann Talking Doll	7⅞ x 11

MANUFACTURER/MARKING
1972 Montgomery Ward

ITEM	SIZE
Advertisement - Raggedy Ann and Andy 1998 Collectible Ornament	4⅞ x 5⅛

MANUFACTURER/MARKING
Raggedy Ann and Andy 1998 Simon & Schuster, Inc.

ITEM	SIZE
Advertisement - Raggedy Ann and Andy 2000 Festival in Japan program (English)	5 x 7

MANUFACTURER/MARKING
Simon & Schuster, Inc., licensed by United Media

ITEM

Advertisement - Raggedy Ann and Andy 2000 Festival in Japan program (Japanese)

SIZE

4¼ x 5½

MANUFACTURER/MARKING

ITEM

Advertisement - Raggedy Ann and Andy and the Camel with the Wrinkled Knees Pop-up Book

SIZE

6⅞ x 9¼

MANUFACTURER/MARKING

$19.95 plus shipping

ITEM

Advertisement - Raggedy Ann and Andy and the Camel with the Wrinkled Knees Story

SIZE

2¾ x 4¼

MANUFACTURER/MARKING

R. John Wright Dolls, Inc., Bennington, VT, Simon & Schuster, Inc., licensed by United Media

ITEM

Advertisement - Raggedy Ann and Andy appliqued linen towels

SIZE

8¾ x 12⅛

MANUFACTURER/MARKING

Home and Garden, Carole Stupell Ltd., 507 Madison Avenue, New York 22 #946

ITEM	SIZE
Advertisement - Raggedy Ann and Andy Authentic Doll Certificate of Authenticity	5 x 7

MANUFACTURER/MARKING
Classic Raggedy Ann and Andy, Joni Gruelle, Granddaughter of Johnny Gruelle, Applause

ITEM	SIZE
Advertisement - Raggedy Ann and Andy Box Set Dolls with Certificate of Authenticity	7⅞ x 10⅜

MANUFACTURER/MARKING
Item No: 877359018

ITEM	SIZE
Advertisement - Raggedy Ann and Andy Camper	8⅛ x 11

MANUFACTURER/MARKING

ITEM	SIZE
Advertisement - Raggedy Ann and Andy Christmas Ornaments from The Danbury Mint	8½ x 11

MANUFACTURER/MARKING
Simon & Schuster, Inc., licensed by United Media, MBI-AA0/bro

ITEM

Advertisement - Raggedy Ann and Andy Christmas Ornaments Reservation Application

SIZE

5½ x 8½

MANUFACTURER/MARKING

Simon & Schuster, Inc., licensed by United Media, MBI-AAO/oc

ITEM

Advertisement - Raggedy Ann and Andy Christmas Tree

SIZE

8½ x 11

MANUFACTURER/MARKING

Simon & Schuster, Inc., licensed by United Media, MBI, 9141:bro

ITEM

Advertisement - Raggedy Ann and Andy Christmas Tree Reservation Application

SIZE

5½ x 8½

MANUFACTURER/MARKING

Simon & Schuster, Inc., licensed by United Media, MBI, 9141:OC

ITEM

Advertisement - Raggedy Ann and Andy Cross Stitch Workshop

SIZE

5½ x 8½

MANUFACTURER/MARKING

Thursday, June 6, 2002

ITEM	SIZE
Advertisement - Raggedy Ann and Andy Crystal Ornaments Reservation Application	7½ x 12½

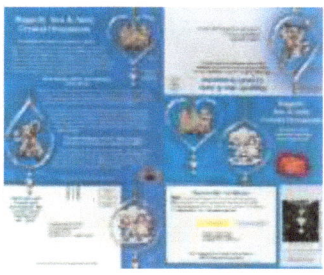

MANUFACTURER/MARKING
Simon & Schuster, Inc., licensed by United Media, MBI, 9484/SM 039915717215

ITEM	SIZE
Advertisement - Raggedy Ann and Andy Dolls from The Danbury Mint Reservation Application	5½ x 11⅛

MANUFACTURER/MARKING
The Danbury Mint © Simon & Schuster, Inc., licensed by United Media 4M32 Christmas, Halloween, Sweet Valentines, Patriotic Pair

ITEM	SIZE
Advertisement - Raggedy Ann and Andy Floating Toys	2⅞ x 5⅞

MANUFACTURER/MARKING
Citroen's Art Gallery, 225 Fifth Avenue, New York, 10, New York

ITEM	SIZE
Advertisement - Raggedy Ann and Andy Gathering a Bouquet Collector Figurine Introduction	8½ x 11

MANUFACTURER/MARKING
1998 Simon & Schuster, Inc., AAF:MI

ITEM	SIZE
Advertisement - Raggedy Ann and Andy Gathering a Bouquet Collector Figurine Reservation Application	5½ x 8½

MANUFACTURER/MARKING
1998 Simon & Schuster, Inc., AAF:OC, The Danbury Mint © MBI, Simon & Schuster, Inc., licensed by United Media

ITEM	SIZE
Advertisement - Raggedy Ann and Andy Gathering a Bouquet Collector Figurine Reservation Application	5⅝ x 7⅞

MANUFACTURER/MARKING
The Danbury Mint © MBI, Simon & Schuster, Inc., licensed by United Media

ITEM	SIZE
Advertisement - Raggedy Ann and Andy Glitter Ornaments Credit Voucher	8½ x 11

MANUFACTURER/MARKING
Simon & Schuster, Inc., licensed by United Media

ITEM	SIZE
Advertisement - Raggedy Ann and Andy Glitter Ornaments Reservation Application	7½ x 12½

MANUFACTURER/MARKING
Simon & Schuster, Inc., licensed by United Media, MBI 94831SM

ITEM	SIZE
Advertisement - Raggedy Ann and Andy leaning against a wooden cradle	3¼ x 6½

MANUFACTURER/MARKING
2000 CROCS Limited Partnership 7/12/00-8/27/00

ITEM	SIZE
Advertisement - Raggedy Ann and Andy Make Their Check Debut	8½ x 11

MANUFACTURER/MARKING
Image Checks

ITEM	SIZE
Advertisement - Raggedy Ann and Andy Now Appearing at Raggedy Ann and Andy's Playroom	18½ x 11

MANUFACTURER/MARKING
Located at Once Upon A Time...books for kids

ITEM	SIZE
Advertisement - Raggedy Ann and Andy or Friends and Friends and Friends Program, by Jeffrey Sanzel and Kevin F. Story	8½ x 11

MANUFACTURER/MARKING
Theatre Three, 412 Main Street, Port Jefferson, NY 11777, Saturday, July 13, 2024, 11:00 a.m.

ITEM	SIZE
Advertisement - Raggedy Ann and Andy Ornament Reservation Certificate	4 x 5⅝

MANUFACTURER/MARKING

9718902688 9480017DOLL

ITEM	SIZE
Advertisement - Raggedy Ann and Andy Ornament Statement of Authenticity	7¼ x 9⅝

MANUFACTURER/MARKING

ITEM	SIZE
Advertisement - Raggedy Ann and Andy Ornaments and Keepsake Box	4 x 6¼

MANUFACTURER/MARKING

Simon & Schuster, Inc., licensed by United Media

ITEM	SIZE
Advertisement - Raggedy Ann and Andy Plaques and Clock	7½ x 10⅞

MANUFACTURER/MARKING

H.M. Specialties, 250 West 55th Street, New York, New York 10019

ITEM | SIZE
Advertisement - Raggedy Ann and Andy Prepare for New Home | 8½ x 11

MANUFACTURER/MARKING
Pat Monahan Partners

ITEM | SIZE
Advertisement - Raggedy Ann and Andy Rally Happy Card | 2½ x 4½

MANUFACTURER/MARKING
June 10, 11, 2016, Arcola, IL, The Cheery Scarecrow

ITEM | SIZE
Advertisement - Raggedy Ann and Andy Sculptures Certificate of Registration | 3⅜ x 6⅜

MANUFACTURER/MARKING
Simon & Schuster, Inc., A807 ™

ITEM | SIZE
Advertisement - Raggedy Ann and Andy Sleigh Reservation Application | 8½ x 11

MANUFACTURER/MARKING
MBI 9141/f2

ITEM

Advertisement - Raggedy Ann and Andy Stacking Set Certificate of Authenticity

SIZE

3½ x 8⅜

MANUFACTURER/MARKING

22nd Anniversary 2008, #900

ITEM

Advertisement - Raggedy Ann and Andy Stick On Set

SIZE

4⅞ x 8¼

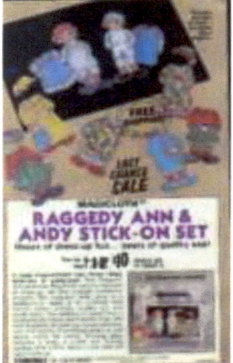

MANUFACTURER/MARKING

Stock No. 11-76997-3

ITEM

Advertisement - Raggedy Ann and Andy Sweet Valentines Dolls

SIZE

8½ x 11

MANUFACTURER/MARKING

Simon & Schuster, Inc., licensed by United Media, MBI, 8862/bro

ITEM

Advertisement - Raggedy Ann and Andy Sweet Valentines Dolls Posing Instructions

SIZE

4¼ x 8½

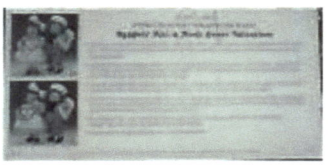

MANUFACTURER/MARKING

ITEM

Advertisement - Raggedy Ann and Andy Sweet Valentines Dolls Reservation Application

SIZE

5½ x 8½

MANUFACTURER/MARKING

Simon & Schuster, Inc., licensed by United Media, MBI, 8862/oc

ITEM

Advertisement - Raggedy Ann and Andy Tea Set

SIZE

8⅛ x 11

MANUFACTURER/MARKING

ITEM

Advertisement - Raggedy Ann and Andy Treasure Craft Limited Edition Gallery Cookie Jar Certificate of Authenticity

SIZE

5¾ x 7¾

MANUFACTURER/MARKING

Paul E. Helgesen, President, Treasure Craft 550 of 1,000

ITEM

Advertisement - Raggedy Ann and Andy Walk, Arcola, Illinois, May 18, 2002

SIZE

8½ x 11

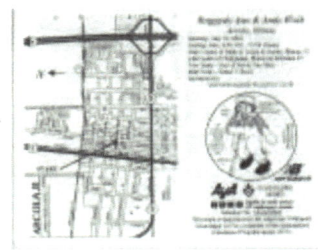

MANUFACTURER/MARKING

American Volkssport Association (AVA)

ITEM	SIZE
Advertisement - Raggedy Ann and Andy Walk, Arcola, Illinois, May 19, 2001	8½ x 11

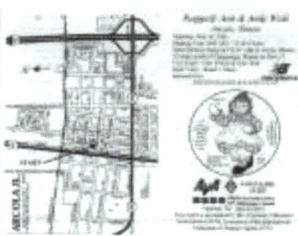

MANUFACTURER/MARKING
American Volkssport Association (AVA)

ITEM	SIZE
Advertisement - Raggedy Ann and Andy: Johnny Gruelle's Dolls with Heart Video	6 x 16

MANUFACTURER/MARKING
Sirocco Productions, Inc.

ITEM	SIZE
Advertisement - Raggedy Ann and Andy's Hospital Visiting Program	9 x 15

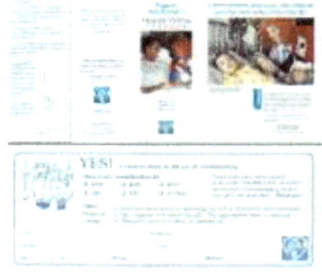

MANUFACTURER/MARKING
Macmillan, Inc., Love Yourself Foundation

ITEM	SIZE
Advertisement - Raggedy Ann and Andy's Long Island Adventure	8½ x 11

MANUFACTURER/MARKING
Wednesday, May 15, 1996

ITEM	SIZE
Advertisement - Raggedy Ann and Andy's Long Island Adventure Program	5½ x 8½

MANUFACTURER/MARKING

1996 Linda L. Pytko

ITEM	SIZE
Advertisement - Raggedy Ann and Andy's Preschool Play House and Rag Dolls in 7 Sizes	8½ x 11

MANUFACTURER/MARKING

ITEM	SIZE
Advertisement - Raggedy Ann and Andy's Storytime Club	9½ x 12½

MANUFACTURER/MARKING

Contained in Better Homes & Gardens Magazine, July 1967

ITEM	SIZE
Advertisement - Raggedy Ann and Raggedy Andy Dishes, Lamps and Clothes Hangers	8⅛ x 11

MANUFACTURER/MARKING

1974 The Bobbs-Merrill Co., Inc., J.C. Penney

ITEM	SIZE
Advertisement - Raggedy Ann and Raggedy Andy Georgene Limited Edition Japanese Reproduction Set, certificate of authenticity	4 x 6

MANUFACTURER/MARKING

Axcis, Inc., 2001 Applause, LLC 083361626423, #0964 of 4,000

ITEM	SIZE
Advertisement - Raggedy Ann and Raggedy Andy Gift Items	8⅛ x 10½

MANUFACTURER/MARKING

ITEM	SIZE
Advertisement - Raggedy Ann and Raggedy Andy rubber stamps for the Japanese market	8½ x 11

MANUFACTURER/MARKING

© Simon & Schuster, Inc., licensed by United Media 2000

ITEM	SIZE
Advertisement - Raggedy Ann and Raggedy Andy Spinning Top, Colorforms and Colorola	8⅛ x 11

MANUFACTURER/MARKING

1974 The Bobbs-Merrill Co., Inc., J.C. Penney

ITEM	SIZE
Advertisement - Raggedy Ann and Skippy the Sailor watches	8½ x 11

MANUFACTURER/MARKING
1974 Spiegel

ITEM	SIZE
Advertisement - Raggedy Ann Broadway Musical Revival Effort	8½ x 11

MANUFACTURER/MARKING

ITEM	SIZE
Advertisement - Raggedy Ann Cookbook Entry	8½ x 11

MANUFACTURER/MARKING

ITEM	SIZE
Advertisement - Raggedy Ann Craft Doll by Russ Toy	8½ x 11

MANUFACTURER/MARKING
Country Living, September 2005

ITEM | SIZE
Advertisement - Raggedy Ann Doll Patent | 3¾ x 8½

MANUFACTURER/MARKING
1915-2015

ITEM | SIZE
Advertisement - Raggedy Ann Festival Downtown Cynthiana, KY, April 16, 2011 | 8½ x 11

MANUFACTURER/MARKING
9:00 a.m.-4:00 p.m., Simon & Schuster, Inc., licensed by Peanuts Worldwide, LLC

ITEM | SIZE
Advertisement - Raggedy Ann Festival Downtown Cynthiana, KY, April 17, 2010 | 8½ x 11

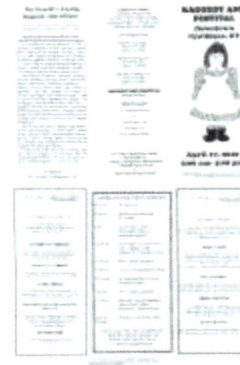

MANUFACTURER/MARKING
Simon & Schuster, Inc., licensed by United Media, 9:00 a.m.-4:00 p.m.

ITEM | SIZE
Advertisement - Raggedy Ann Festival Downtown Cynthiana, KY, April 2009 | 8½ x 11

MANUFACTURER/MARKING
Every Year, Third Saturday in April, 9:00 a.m. to 4:00 p.m.

ITEM

Advertisement - Raggedy Ann Festival, Flat Run Veterans' Park, Cynthiana, KY, April 21, 2012

SIZE

3¾ x 8½

MANUFACTURER/MARKING

9:00 a.m. to 4: 00 p.m.

ITEM

Advertisement - Raggedy Ann grooming doll and battery-powered hair untangler

SIZE

8½ x 11

MANUFACTURER/MARKING

1974 Spiegel

ITEM

Advertisement - Raggedy Ann highchair

SIZE

8½ x 11

MANUFACTURER/MARKING

1974 Spiegel

ITEM

Advertisement - Raggedy Ann Posing Instructions

SIZE

4⅛ x 8½

MANUFACTURER/MARKING

MBI, 8428/UPC

ITEM

Advertisement - Raggedy Ann Rally at Rockome, June 2014 Song Lyrics

SIZE

8½ x 11

MANUFACTURER/MARKING

Raggedy Ann Rally, Patty Hall

ITEM

Advertisement - Raggedy Ann Rally at Rockome, June 7, 2014 Schedule of Events

SIZE

8½ x 11

MANUFACTURER/MARKING

Rekindling the Friendship, Planning session for 2015

ITEM

Advertisement - Raggedy Ann Rally Featuring Percy Policeman and the Nice Fat Policeman Program and Menu

SIZE

8½ x 11

MANUFACTURER/MARKING

ITEM

Advertisement - Raggedy Ann Rally Schedule of Events, heart border

SIZE

8½ x 11

MANUFACTURER/MARKING

Thursday, June 9-Saturday, June 11, 2016

ITEM | SIZE
Advertisement - Raggedy Ann Rally Schedule of Events, June 8-10, 2017 | 8½ x 11

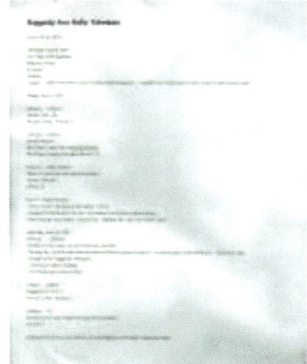

MANUFACTURER/MARKING

ITEM | SIZE
Advertisement - Raggedy Ann Rally Sharing the Love Raggedy Style Schedule of Events | 8½ x 11

MANUFACTURER/MARKING

ITEM | SIZE
Advertisement - Raggedy Ann Rally Welcome Banquet and Auction Program, June 10, 2016 | 5½ x 8½

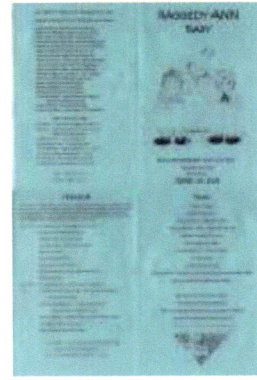

MANUFACTURER/MARKING

ITEM | SIZE
Advertisement - Raggedy Ann Rally Welcome Banquet and Auction Program, June 12, 2015 | 2¾ x 4⅞

MANUFACTURER/MARKING

Happy 100th Birthday, June 12, 2015, 6:00 p.m.

ITEM

Advertisement - Raggedy Ann Rally Welcome Banquet and Auction Program, June 6, 2014

SIZE

8½ x 11

MANUFACTURER/MARKING

Joni Gruelle 2014

ITEM

Advertisement - Raggedy Ann Rally Welcome Banquet and Auction Program, June 9, 2017

SIZE

5½ x 8½

MANUFACTURER/MARKING

Yoder's Kitchen, Arthur, IL, Raggedy Ann, Raggedy Andy and Sunny Bunny

ITEM

Advertisement - Raggedy Ann Rally, Welcome Dinner and Auction Place Card, Celebrating Cheery Scarecrow

SIZE

2⅝ x 5⅝

MANUFACTURER/MARKING

June 10, 2016, 6:00 p.m.

ITEM

Advertisement - Raggedy Ann sitting on a bed showing a Tidewater Traders comforter

SIZE

3 x 5

MANUFACTURER/MARKING

ITEM	SIZE
Advertisement - Raggedy Ann sitting on a white night stand	7¼ x 7½

MANUFACTURER/MARKING

$34.99 Twin size reversible comforter

ITEM	SIZE
Advertisement - Raggedy Ann Slumber Bag/Comforter	8½ x 11

MANUFACTURER/MARKING

1988 Macmillan, Inc. 049643715132

ITEM	SIZE
Advertisement - Raggedy Ann Sugar Plum Doll, Certificate of Authenticity	3⅜ x 6⅛

MANUFACTURER/MARKING

#252 of 5,000

ITEM	SIZE
Advertisement - Raggedy Ann, Inner World	3 x 6

MANUFACTURER/MARKING

ITEM

Advertisement - Raggedy Ann's 100th Birthday Party Gala Schedule of Events

SIZE

3 x 5⅝

MANUFACTURER/MARKING

June 13, 2015

ITEM

Advertisement - Raggedy Ann's 100th Birthday Party Gala Schedule of Events, black and white

SIZE

8½ x 11

MANUFACTURER/MARKING

Saturday, June 13, 2015, 6:00 p.m.

ITEM

Advertisement - Raggedy Ann's 100th Birthday Party Gala Schedule of Events, color

SIZE

8½ x 11

MANUFACTURER/MARKING

Saturday, June 13, 2015, 6:00 p.m.

ITEM

Advertisement - Raggedy Ann's 90th Birthday Essay Contest

SIZE

8½ x 11

MANUFACTURER/MARKING

© Simon & Schuster, Inc., licensed by United Media

ITEM	SIZE
Advertisement - Raggedy Ann's 95th Anniversary Doll Certificate of Authenticity	4¾ x 7½

MANUFACTURER/MARKING
Simon & Schuster, Inc., licensed by United Media, 2010 Alexander Doll Co., Inc., Gale Jarvis, President #46/150

ITEM	SIZE
Advertisement - Raggedy Ann's Bed, The Magical Hour, by R. John Wright Dolls Certificate of Authenticity	2½ x 4

MANUFACTURER/MARKING
#161/250 R. John Wright Dolls, Inc., Bennington, VT, Simon & Schuster, Inc., licensed by United Media, Year of Issue: 2004

ITEM	SIZE
Advertisement - Raggedy Friends Gathering Open House at 247 West Main Street, Arcola	8½ x 11

MANUFACTURER/MARKING
Susie Patridge Downsizing 44 years of collecting

ITEM	SIZE
Advertisement - Raggedy Land 12th Annual Raggedy Ann and Andy Festival Items	8½ x 11

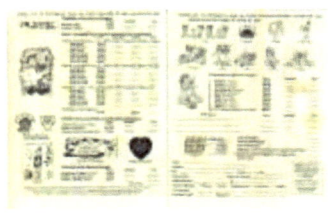

MANUFACTURER/MARKING

ITEM	SIZE
Advertisement - Raggedy Land Baby and Juvenile Bedding, Shylling Items, Mattel Dolls and Street Signs	8½ x 11

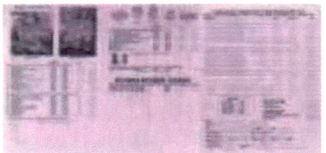

MANUFACTURER/MARKING
Simon & Schuster, Inc., licensed by United Media

ITEM	SIZE
Advertisement - Raggedy Land Enesco Spring and Christmas Figurines and Kurt S. Adler Ornaments for 2000	8½ x 11

MANUFACTURER/MARKING
Simon & Schuster, Inc., licensed by United Media

ITEM	SIZE
Advertisement - Raggedy Land Rubber Stamps, Cling/Sticker, Throw	8½ x 11

MANUFACTURER/MARKING
Simon & Schuster, Inc., licensed by United Media

ITEM	SIZE
Advertisement - Raggedy Land Rubber Stamps, License Plate Holder, Deck of Playing Cards, Coloring Pages	8½ x 11

MANUFACTURER/MARKING
© Simon & Schuster, Inc., licensed by United Media

ITEM	SIZE
Advertisement - Raggedy Land, Patricia Hall and Raggedy Ann and Andy Museum	8½ x 11

MANUFACTURER/MARKING

ITEM	SIZE
Advertisement - Raggedy Mixer 2016	8½ x 11

MANUFACTURER/MARKING

ITEM	SIZE
Advertisement - Raggedy Money, $10	2½ x 6

MANUFACTURER/MARKING

BL00002040A

ITEM	SIZE
Advertisement - Raggedy Twins Radio	8½ x 11

MANUFACTURER/MARKING

1974 Spiegel

ITEM	SIZE
Advertisement - Raggedy, A Documentary Film - The Magical Legacy of Johnny Gruelle, black and white	4¼ x 11

MANUFACTURER/MARKING
www.indiegogo.com/raggedyann

ITEM	SIZE
Advertisement - Raggedy, a Documentary Film - The Magical Legacy of Johnny Gruelle, color	4¼ x 11

MANUFACTURER/MARKING
A Common Sense Films Production in association with BEP Communications, www.indigogo.com/raggedyann

ITEM	SIZE
Advertisement - Raggedys and Teddys Gold Trimmed Merchandise Order Form	8½ x 11

MANUFACTURER/MARKING

ITEM	SIZE
Advertisement - Rags Newsletter and The Johnny Gruelle Raggedy Ann and Andy Museum, lavender, Castle Press	8½ x 11

MANUFACTURER/MARKING

ITEM

Advertisement - Rags Newsletter and The Johnny Gruelle Raggedy Ann and Andy Museum, pink, Rankin Publishing

SIZE

8½ x 11

MANUFACTURER/MARKING

ITEM

Advertisement - Rags Newsletter and The Johnny Gruelle Raggedy Ann and Andy Museum, yellow, Rankin Publishing

SIZE

8½ x 11

MANUFACTURER/MARKING

ITEM

Advertisement - Ralston Purina

SIZE

6½ x 7¾

MANUFACTURER/MARKING

March 1931 Good Housekeeping, Good Night Daddy!

ITEM

Advertisement - Reading Makes Friends

SIZE

6⅞ x 10⅜

MANUFACTURER/MARKING

Mulberry Books

ITEM
Advertisement - Rest Mats and Cots

SIZE
5¾ x 7⅛

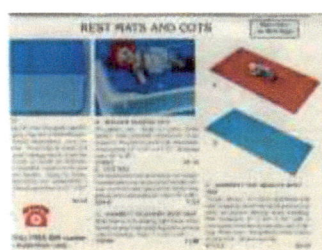

MANUFACTURER/MARKING
Thomas L. Clark Manufacturing Company

ITEM
Advertisement - Restfoam, girl sleeping with Raggedy Ann

SIZE
10 x 13

MANUFACTURER/MARKING
1953 Hewitt-Robins Incorporated, Buffalo, N.Y.

ITEM
Advertisement - Rhymes for Kindly Children

SIZE
4¾ x 9½

MANUFACTURER/MARKING
P.F. Volland & Co.

ITEM
Advertisement - Rosemarie and Ronald Certificate of Adoption

SIZE
3⅛ x 3¾

MANUFACTURER/MARKING
2000 Priscilla Hillman, Simon & Schuster, Inc., Enesco Corp., Cherished Teddies 045544709576 706981, IC4/800

ITEM | SIZE
Advertisement - Santa's Special Delivery Certificate of Ownership | 4½ x 6½

MANUFACTURER/MARKING

1998 Hasbro, Inc. A1147

ITEM | SIZE
Advertisement - Santa's Special Delivery Posing Instructions | 5½ x 8½

MANUFACTURER/MARKING

1998 Hasbro, Inc., SAR/1pc

ITEM | SIZE
Advertisement - Santa's Special Delivery poster | 14½ x 17⅛

MANUFACTURER/MARKING

1998 Hasbro, Inc., SAR/bro

ITEM | SIZE
Advertisement - Santa's Special Delivery Reservation Application | 7¼ x 11¾

MANUFACTURER/MARKING

SAR/SLF The Danbury Mint

ITEM

Advertisement - Santa's Special Delivery Reservation Application, with prefilled address

SIZE

5½ x 8½

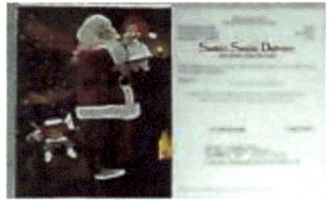

MANUFACTURER/MARKING

1998 Hasbro, Inc., SAR/bro

ITEM

Advertisement - Scatter Seeds of Happiness Wherever You May Go Certificate of Authenticity

SIZE

3¼ x 7⅜

MANUFACTURER/MARKING

Simon & Schuster, Inc., licensed by United Media, Enesco Corp. 106217 045544550390

ITEM

Advertisement - Schmid 1980 Editions, The Sunshine Peddler/First Run

SIZE

8½ x 11

MANUFACTURER/MARKING

1978, 1980 The Bobbs-Merrill Co., Inc., Schmid Bros., Inc.

ITEM

Advertisement - Schmid 1981 Editions, The Raggedy Shuffle/Snowtime Frolic

SIZE

8½ x 11

MANUFACTURER/MARKING

1978, 1980, 1981, 1982 The Bobbs-Merrill Co., Inc., Schmid Bros., Inc.

ITEM	SIZE
Advertisement - Schmid 1982 Editions, Flying High	8½ x 11

MANUFACTURER/MARKING

1978, 1980, 1981, 1982, 1983 The Bobbs-Merrill Co., Inc., Schmid Bros., Inc.

ITEM	SIZE
Advertisement - Schmid 1983 Editions, Winning Streak	8½ x 11

MANUFACTURER/MARKING

1983 The Bobbs-Merrill Co., Inc., Schmid Bros., Inc.

ITEM	SIZE
Advertisement - Schmid Cartoon Series for 1979	3 x 6

MANUFACTURER/MARKING

1979 The Bobbs-Merrill Co., Inc., Schmid Bros., Inc.

ITEM	SIZE
Advertisement - School Days are Fun Days Certificate of Authenticity	3¼ x 7⅜

MANUFACTURER/MARKING

Simon & Schuster, Inc., licensed by United Media, Enesco Corp. 045544394710 291773

ITEM	SIZE
Advertisement - Scot Tissue	3½ x 5

MANUFACTURER/MARKING

ITEM	SIZE
Advertisement - Service for four plus cook and serve accessories	8½ x 11

MANUFACTURER/MARKING

1974 Spiegel

ITEM	SIZE
Advertisement - Serving up a Helping of Kindness Certificate of Authenticity	3¼ x 7⅜

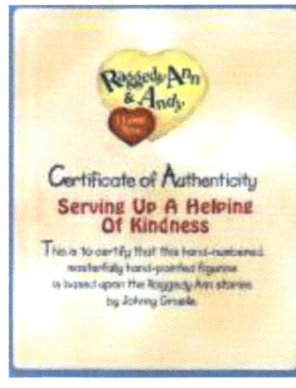

MANUFACTURER/MARKING

Simon & Schuster, Inc., licensed by United Media, Enesco Corp. 045544760188 953156

ITEM	SIZE
Advertisement - Sharing a Basket Full of Kindness Certificate of Authenticity	3¼ x 7⅜

MANUFACTURER/MARKING

Simon & Schuster, Inc., licensed by United Media, Enesco Corp. 045544759403 953024

ITEM | SIZE
Advertisement - Sheets in a patchprint motif | 8½ x 11

MANUFACTURER/MARKING

1974 Spiegel

ITEM | SIZE
Advertisement - Sheraton Hotels | 10 x 13

MANUFACTURER/MARKING

Sheraton Corp., Look May 26, 1959, Family Plan-Children Free

ITEM | SIZE
Advertisement - Ships Ahoy Collector Registration Card | 4 x 5½

MANUFACTURER/MARKING

2007 Alexander Doll Co. A1575437

ITEM | SIZE
Advertisement - Ships Ahoy Raggedy Ann 95th Anniversary Doll Certificate of Authenticity | 4¾ x 7½

MANUFACTURER/MARKING

2010 Alexander Doll Co., Inc. #88/150, Gale Jarvis, President

ITEM	SIZE
Advertisement - Simmons Juvenile Products Company, Inc.	8½ x 11

MANUFACTURER/MARKING

1993 Macmillan, Inc.

ITEM	SIZE
Advertisement - Simplicity 8043, Dolls available in sizes 15", 26" and 36"	8½ x 11

MANUFACTURER/MARKING

© Simon & Schuster, Inc., licensed by United Media

ITEM	SIZE
Advertisement - Sleepytime Raggedy Ann, 12" and 17" dolls	5¾ x 7½

MANUFACTURER/MARKING

ITEM	SIZE
Advertisement - Smiles and Happiness are Truly Catching Certificate of Authenticity	3¼ x 7⅜

MANUFACTURER/MARKING

1999 Simon & Schuster, Inc., Enesco Corp. 544892 98RA598

ITEM	SIZE
Advertisement - Smokey Bear and Raggedy Ann Now Live Under the Same Roof	8¼ x 11¼

MANUFACTURER/MARKING

1971 Knickerbocker Toy Co., Inc., March 1971 Playthings

ITEM	SIZE
Advertisement - Snodgrass Sales	7¾ x 10⅛

MANUFACTURER/MARKING

Applause, LLC

ITEM	SIZE
Advertisement - Snowden and Friends Color Change Cup	1⅞ x 5

MANUFACTURER/MARKING

Snowden 1998 Dayton Hudson Corp., Raggedy Ann and Andy 1998 Simon & Schuster, Inc.

ITEM	SIZE
Advertisement - Snowden and Friends Goodie Bag	3 x 7

MANUFACTURER/MARKING

1998 Snowden Dayton Hudson Corp., Raggedy Ann and Andy, Simon & Schuster, Inc.

ITEM	SIZE
Advertisement - So Much to do When you Turn Two Certificate of Authenticity	3¼ x 7⅜

MANUFACTURER/MARKING

Simon & Schuster, Inc., licensed by United Media, Enesco Corp. 045544404266 823716

ITEM	SIZE
Advertisement - Something Special from Montgomery Ward	8½ x 11

MANUFACTURER/MARKING

1978/1980 The Bobbs-Merrill Company, Inc., 18-50118 Pillow Set, #277 Blue Tango

ITEM	SIZE
Advertisement - Spend Life in Kindness Making New Friends Certificate of Authenticity	3¼ x 7⅜

MANUFACTURER/MARKING

Simon & Schuster, Inc., licensed by United Media, Enesco Corp. 045544679794 677760

ITEM	SIZE
Advertisement - Stephens Publishing Company	4⅜ x 5⅝

MANUFACTURER/MARKING

September 1948 Playthings

ITEM	SIZE
Advertisement - Stocking Stuffers	8⅛ x 11

MANUFACTURER/MARKING
1974 The Bobbs-Merrill Co., Inc., J.C. Penney

ITEM	SIZE
Advertisement - Stocking Up on Christmas Cheer Certificate of Authenticity	3¼ x 7⅜

MANUFACTURER/MARKING
Simon & Schuster, Inc., licensed by United Media, Enesco Corp. 045544272834 104403

ITEM	SIZE
Advertisement - Sunny Bunny Welcomes You to the Raggedy Ann Rally Banquet and Silent Auction	3⅝ x 5

MANUFACTURER/MARKING
Yoder's Kitchen, Arthur, IL

ITEM	SIZE
Advertisement - Survey for future Raggedy Ann rallies	5½ x 8⅝

MANUFACTURER/MARKING

ITEM	SIZE
Advertisement - Take a Letter...You're a Special Friend Certificate of Authenticity	3¼ x 7⅜

MANUFACTURER/MARKING

Simon & Schuster, Inc., licensed by United Media, Enesco Corp. 045544389785 289353

ITEM	SIZE
Advertisement - Talon Fastener	10¼ x 11¼

MANUFACTURER/MARKING

August 1948 - Ladies Home Journal

ITEM	SIZE
Advertisement - Target the Family: Gifts from the Heart	18 x 10¾

MANUFACTURER/MARKING

ITEM	SIZE
Advertisement - Target the Family: Hand in Hand Through the Holidays	18 x 10¾

MANUFACTURER/MARKING

Target the Family

ITEM	SIZE
Advertisement - Tea for Two with Me and You Certificate of Authenticity	3¼ x 7⅜

MANUFACTURER/MARKING
Simon & Schuster, Inc., licensed by United Media, Enesco Corp. 045544319973 832030

ITEM	SIZE
Advertisement - Tea Time Certificate of Authenticity	3¾ x 6⅝

MANUFACTURER/MARKING
1998 Simon & Schuster, Inc. A807

ITEM	SIZE
Advertisement - Tea Time Sculpture	8½ x 11

MANUFACTURER/MARKING
1998 Simon & Schuster, Inc., AAF:ba ™

ITEM	SIZE
Advertisement - Thank You for Attending Walk	8½ x 11

MANUFACTURER/MARKING

ITEM

Advertisement - The 12th Annual Raggedy Ann and Andy Festival Premiere of Arcola Raggedy Ann Doll

SIZE

5⅜ x 8½

MANUFACTURER/MARKING

May 18-20, 2001

ITEM

Advertisement - The 13th Original Raggedy Ann and Andy Festival

SIZE

5½ x 8½

MANUFACTURER/MARKING

May 18 and 19, 2002, Arcola, Illinois

ITEM

Advertisement - The 13th Original Raggedy Ann and Andy Festival Donation Receipt

SIZE

4¼ x 11

MANUFACTURER/MARKING

Magnets, Washcloth, Musical Rag Doll - $72.00

ITEM

Advertisement - The 13th Original Raggedy Ann and Andy Festival Free Concerts

SIZE

5⅝ x 8½

MANUFACTURER/MARKING

Duke Tumatoe and the Power Trio, Ginny Owens

ITEM	SIZE
Advertisement - The 14th Original Raggedy Ann and Andy Festival	8½ x 11

MANUFACTURER/MARKING
May 17-18, 2003, Arcola, Illinois

ITEM	SIZE
Advertisement - The 15th Original Raggedy Ann and Andy Festival Limited Edition Doll	8½ x 11

MANUFACTURER/MARKING
May 22 and 23, 2004

ITEM	SIZE
Advertisement - The 15th Original Raggedy Ann and Andy Festival Program	5½ x 8½

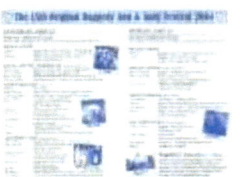

MANUFACTURER/MARKING
May 22-23, 2004, Arcola, IL

ITEM	SIZE
Advertisement - The 15th Original Raggedy Ann and Andy Festival Schedule of Events Events	8½ x 11

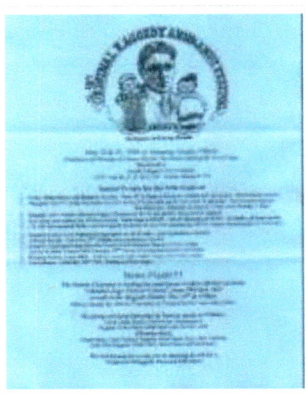

MANUFACTURER/MARKING
May 22-23, 2004, Arcola, IL

ITEM

Advertisement - The 16th Original Raggedy Ann and Andy Festival Parade Route

SIZE

8½ x 11

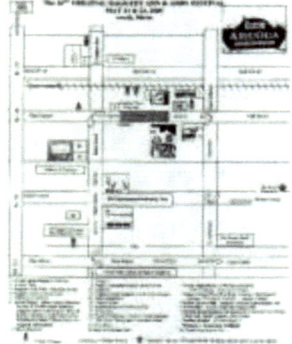

MANUFACTURER/MARKING

May 21 and 22, 2005, Arcola, IL

ITEM

Advertisement - The 16th Original Raggedy Ann and Andy Festival Schedule of Events

SIZE

8½ x 11

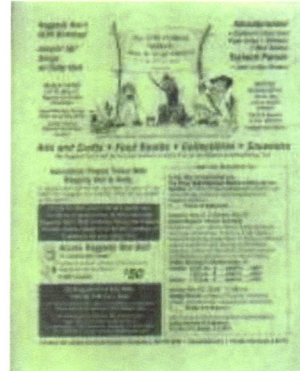

MANUFACTURER/MARKING

May 21 and 22, 2005

ITEM

Advertisement - The 16th Original Raggedy Ann and Andy Festival Schedule of Events

SIZE

5½ x 8½

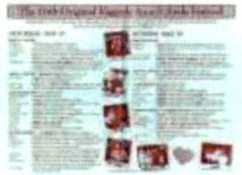

MANUFACTURER/MARKING

May 20-22, 2005, Arcola, IL

ITEM

Advertisement - The 17th Original Raggedy Ann and Andy Festival Schedule of Events

SIZE

5½ x 8½

MANUFACTURER/MARKING

June 9, 10 and 11, 2006

ITEM	SIZE
Advertisement - The 18th Original Raggedy Ann and Andy Festival	5½ x 8½

MANUFACTURER/MARKING	
Arcola Chamber of Commerce	

ITEM	SIZE
Advertisement - The 18th Original Raggedy Ann and Andy Festival Schedule of Events, lavender background	8½ x 11

MANUFACTURER/MARKING	
Emporium Antiques	

ITEM	SIZE
Advertisement - The 18th Original Raggedy Ann and Andy Festival Schedule of Events, white background	8½ x 11

MANUFACTURER/MARKING	
Emporium Antiques	

ITEM	SIZE
Advertisement - The 19th Original Raggedy Ann and Andy Festival	5½ x 8½

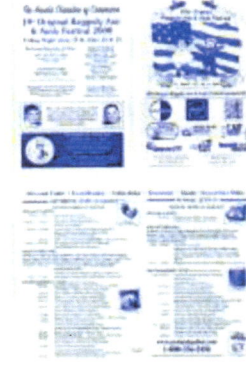

MANUFACTURER/MARKING	
June 13, 14 and 15, 2008	

ITEM

Advertisement - The 2009 Annual Raggedy Ann and Andy Ornament "Bicycle Buddies"

SIZE

5½ x 8½

MANUFACTURER/MARKING

Simon & Schuster, Inc., licensed by United Media 8550-8:cp

ITEM

Advertisement - The 3rd Annual Raggedy Ann and Andy Festival

SIZE

8½ x 11

MANUFACTURER/MARKING

ITEM

Advertisement - The 4th Annual Florida Raggedy Ann, Doll and Teddy Bear Convention

SIZE

5½ x 8½

MANUFACTURER/MARKING

January 26 and 27, 2001

ITEM

Advertisement - The 4th Annual Raggedy Ann and Andy Festival

SIZE

5½ x 8½

MANUFACTURER/MARKING

May 22 and 23, 1993, Arcola, Illinois, birthplace of Johnny Gruelle

ITEM

Advertisement - The 6th Annual Raggedys and Teddys Convention

SIZE

4¼ x 11

MANUFACTURER/MARKING

October 17-18, 2003, Charlotte, North Carolina

ITEM

Advertisement - The 6th Annual Raggedys and Teddys Convention Schedule of Events

SIZE

8½ x 11

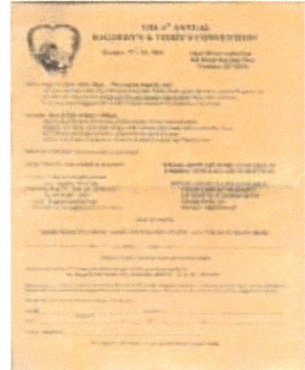

MANUFACTURER/MARKING

October 17-18, 2003, Oasis Shrine Auditorium, Charlotte, NC

ITEM

Advertisement - The 7th Annual Raggedys and Teddys Convention

SIZE

4⅛ x 11

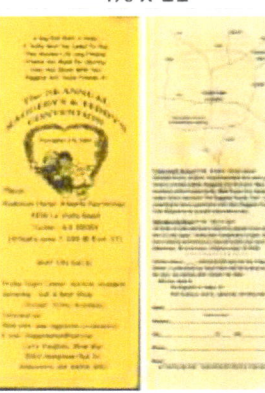

MANUFACTURER/MARKING

November 5-6, 2004, Tucker, Georgia

ITEM

Advertisement - The 8th Annual Raggedy Ann and Raggedy Andy Festival, black art

SIZE

5½ x 8½

MANUFACTURER/MARKING

May 17 and 18, 1997 in Memory of Sue Gruelle

ITEM	SIZE
Advertisement - The 8th Annual Raggedy Ann and Raggedy Andy Festival, red art	3¼ x 4¼

MANUFACTURER/MARKING
So much fun for everyone who loves the Raggedy Ann doll!

ITEM	SIZE
Advertisement - The 8th Annual Raggedy Ann and Raggedy Andy Festival, red art	5½ x 8½

MANUFACTURER/MARKING
May 17 and 18, 1997, In Memory of Sue Gruelle

ITEM	SIZE
Advertisement - The 9th Annual Raggedy Ann and Andy Festival	5½ x 8½

MANUFACTURER/MARKING
May 16 and 17, 1998, In Memory of Worth Gruelle, 1912-1997

ITEM	SIZE
Advertisement - The Adventures of Raggedy Ann and Andy Beastly Ghost Certificate of Authenticity	8½ x 11

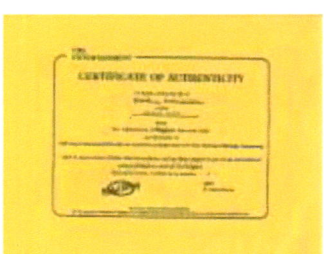

MANUFACTURER/MARKING
#1, Episode 4, Scene 218/G10, CBS, Inc., 1990 Macmillan, Inc.

ITEM	SIZE
Advertisement - The Adventures of Raggedy Ann and Andy Christmas Adventure Certificate of Authenticity	8½ x 11

MANUFACTURER/MARKING	
#1, Episode 9, Scene 306/R10, CBS, Inc., 1990 Macmillan, Inc.	

ITEM	SIZE
Advertisement - The Adventures of Raggedy Ann and Andy Pirate Adventure, Certificate of Authenticity	8½ x 11

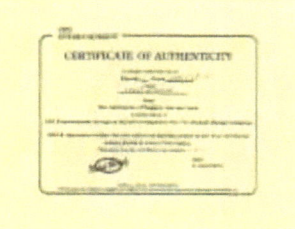

MANUFACTURER/MARKING	
#1, Episode 2, Scene 149/G11, CBS, Inc., 1990 Macmillan, Inc.	

ITEM	SIZE
Advertisement - The Adventures of Raggedy Ann and Andy Warrior Star Adventure Certificate of Authenticity	8½ x 11

MANUFACTURER/MARKING	
#1, Episode 12, Scene 119A/C9, CBS, Inc., 1990 Macmillan, Inc.	

ITEM	SIZE
Advertisement - The Adventures of Raggedy Ann and Andy Warrior Star Adventure Certificate of Authenticity	8½ x 11

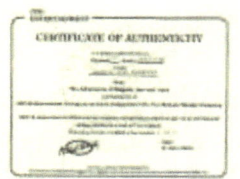

MANUFACTURER/MARKING	
#1, Episode 12, Scene 118/A41, CBS, Inc., 1990 Macmillan, Inc.	

ITEM	SIZE
Advertisement - The Adventures of Raggedy Ann and Andy, The Mabbit Adventure Cel Certificate of Authenticity	8½ x 11

MANUFACTURER/MARKING

Episode 3, Scene 288/A17, CBS, Inc. 1980 Macmillan, Inc.

ITEM	SIZE
Advertisement - The Arcola Chamber of Commerce Welcomes You to Amazing Arcola	3½ x 8½

MANUFACTURER/MARKING

Simon & Schuster, Inc., Joni Gruelle 2002

ITEM	SIZE
Advertisement - The Baby-Sitter Guide, 20 Ways to help make Babysitting Safe & Fun	8½ x 11

MANUFACTURER/MARKING

State of New York, Division of Criminal Justice Services

ITEM	SIZE
Advertisement - The Bank of New York Mortgage Company	11 x 17

MANUFACTURER/MARKING

It takes sophisticated thinking to make mortgages simple.

ITEM	SIZE
Advertisement - The Berry Best Memories are Handmade with Love Certificate of Authenticity	3¼ x 7⅜

MANUFACTURER/MARKING
Simon & Schuster, Inc., licensed by United Media, Enesco Corp. 045544272841 104404

ITEM	SIZE
Advertisement - The Best Things in Life are Free Certificate of Authenticity	3¼ x 7⅜

MANUFACTURER/MARKING
Simon & Schuster, Inc., licensed by United Media, Enesco Corp. 045544759373 953016

ITEM	SIZE
Advertisement - The Camel with the Wrinkled Knees Classic Collectible Pop-up Book	7¾ x 10½

MANUFACTURER/MARKING
Simon & Schuster, Inc., licensed by United Media, Little Simon, ISBN: 0-689-85775-6, 9 780689857751

ITEM	SIZE
Advertisement - The Children's Theatre Company	8½ x 11

MANUFACTURER/MARKING
Kids Store - Montgomery Ward - National Tour 1989-1990

ITEM	SIZE
Advertisement - The Collector's World of Raggedy Ann and Andy Book, Volume I	8½ x 11

MANUFACTURER/MARKING

Theriault's Gold Horse Publishing

ITEM	SIZE
Advertisement - The Collector's World of Raggedy Ann and Andy Book, Volume II	8½ x 11

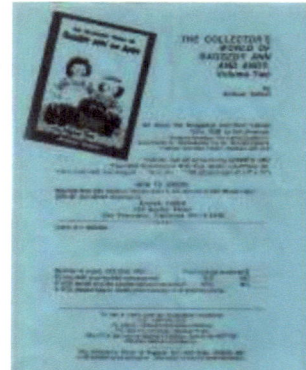

MANUFACTURER/MARKING

Theriault's Gold Horse Publishing

ITEM	SIZE
Advertisement - The Cook's Collection	8½ x 11

MANUFACTURER/MARKING

Raggedy Ann and Andy Cookie Jars, Tea Pot, Sugar Bowl, Creamer, Salt and Pepper Shakers and Magnets

ITEM	SIZE
Advertisement - The Danbury Mint's First Annual Raggedy Ann and Andy Ornament, 2008	8½ x 11

MANUFACTURER/MARKING

Simon & Schuster, Inc., licensed by United Media, MBI 8550-bror

ITEM	SIZE
Advertisement - The Danbury Mint's First Annual Raggedy Ann and Andy Ornament, 2008	7 x 10¾

MANUFACTURER/MARKING
Simon & Schuster, Inc., licensed by United Media

ITEM	SIZE
Advertisement - The Danbury Mint's First Annual Raggedy Ann and Andy Ornament, 2008 Reservation Application	5½ x 8½

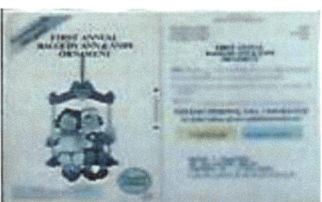

MANUFACTURER/MARKING
Simon & Schuster, Inc., licensed by United Media, MBI 8550:ocr

ITEM	SIZE
Advertisement - The Fabric Mill	8½ x 11

MANUFACTURER/MARKING
Fall 1996 - 1270 Route 110, Farmingdale, NY 11735, 516-752-7660

ITEM	SIZE
Advertisement - The Gift of Happiness Belongs to Those who Unwrap It Certificate of Authenticity	3¼ x 7⅜

MANUFACTURER/MARKING
Simon & Schuster, Inc., licensed by United Media, Enesco Corp. 045544272858 104405

ITEM	SIZE
Advertisement - The Gruelle Family House	8½ x 11

MANUFACTURER/MARKING

537 N. Tacoma Avenue, Indianapolis, Indiana

ITEM	SIZE
Advertisement - The Holiday Show, Long Island's Own Seasonal Spectacular	10 x 14¼

MANUFACTURER/MARKING

Sunday, December 19th at 2:00 p.m.

ITEM	SIZE
Advertisement - The Honest to Goodness Story of Raggedy Andy	8½ x 11

MANUFACTURER/MARKING

Available Spring 2005

ITEM	SIZE
Advertisement - The Last Great Company	8½ x 11

MANUFACTURER/MARKING

1988 Kim Gruelle

ITEM	SIZE
Advertisement - The Last Great Company 1936 Limited Edition Exposition Doll Company Type Reproduction	8½ x 11

MANUFACTURER/MARKING
Kim Gruelle

ITEM	SIZE
Advertisement - The Last Great Company 2000 Limited Edition Holiday Keepsake Raggedy Ann Doll	8½ x 11

MANUFACTURER/MARKING
Kim Gruelle, www.raggedyman.com

ITEM	SIZE
Advertisement - The Last Great Company 80th Anniversary Raggedy Ann and 75th Anniversary Raggedy Andy Limited Edition Dolls for 1995	8½ x 11

MANUFACTURER/MARKING
1995 Applause, LLC, The Last Great Co.

ITEM	SIZE
Advertisement - The Last Great Company Limited Edition Postage Stamp Raggedy Ann Doll for 1997	8½ x 11

MANUFACTURER/MARKING
1997 The Johnny Gruelle Family

ITEM	SIZE
Advertisement - The Last Great Company Original Volland Ann and Andy along with original Volland Ann and Andy books	8½ x 11

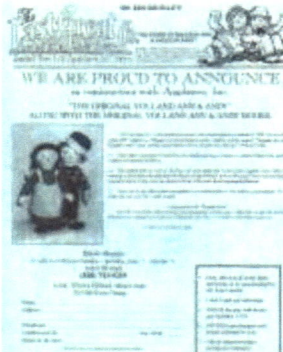

MANUFACTURER/MARKING

Kim Gruelle

ITEM	SIZE
Advertisement - The Last Great Company Raggedy Ann 85th Birthday Last Limited Edition Doll for 1999	8½ x 11

MANUFACTURER/MARKING

Applause, LLC, Hasbro, Inc.

ITEM	SIZE
Advertisement - The Last Great Company Raggedy Ann and Andy Awake/Asleep Limited Edition Dolls for 1996	8½ x 11

MANUFACTURER/MARKING

1996 The Johnny Gruelle Family

ITEM	SIZE
Advertisement - The Last Great Company Raggedy Ann Holiday Doll Limited Edition for 1999	8½ x 11

MANUFACTURER/MARKING

1999 Applause, LLC

ITEM	SIZE
Advertisement - The Last Great Company Raggedy Ann, Andy and Baby Ann Limited Edition Dolls for 1993	8½ x 11

MANUFACTURER/MARKING
1992 Applause, LLC, The Last Great Co.

ITEM	SIZE
Advertisement - The Last Great Company Raggedy Ann, Andy and the Camel with the Wrinkled Knees Limited Edition Dolls for 1994	8½ x 11

MANUFACTURER/MARKING
1994 Applause, LLC, The Last Great Co.

ITEM	SIZE
Advertisement - The Last Great Company Silby Version Georgene Novelty Company Dolls for the 1st Limited Edition of the 21st Century	8½ x 11

MANUFACTURER/MARKING
Simon & Schuster, Inc., Hasbro, Inc., Applause, LLC, Kim Gruelle

ITEM	SIZE
Advertisement - The Last Great Company Storybook Raggedy Ann and Raggedy Andy for 1997 Inspired by Worth Gruelle	8½ x 11

MANUFACTURER/MARKING
The Last Great Co., Kim Gruelle, $69.95 the pair plus $10.25 U.P.S. or $10.50 U.S.P.S. per pair

ITEM	SIZE
Advertisement - The Last Great Company Wishing Pebble Ann and Wishing Stick Andy 2nd Limited Edition Dolls of the 21st Century	8½ x 11

MANUFACTURER/MARKING

Dakin/Applause, Inc.

ITEM	SIZE
Advertisement - The Last Great Company, colored in	8½ x 11

MANUFACTURER/MARKING

Fall 1992

ITEM	SIZE
Advertisement - The More Fun We Give Each Other The More Fun We Each Will Have Certificate of Authenticity	3¼ x 7⅜

MANUFACTURER/MARKING

1999 Simon & Schuster, Inc., Enesco Corp. 597414 93RA238

ITEM	SIZE
Advertisement - The one and only original home of Raggedy Ann and Andy	5½ x 8½

MANUFACTURER/MARKING

ITEM	SIZE
Advertisement - The Raggedy Ann and Andy Glitter Ornament Collection Reservation Application	5½ x 11

MANUFACTURER/MARKING

Simon & Schuster, Inc., licensed by United Media 9483/S

ITEM	SIZE
Advertisement - The Raggedy Ann and Andy Pin Collection Reservation Application	7½ x 12½

MANUFACTURER/MARKING

www.mywillabeeandward.com

ITEM	SIZE
Advertisement - The Raggedy Ann and Andy Throw	11 x 11½

MANUFACTURER/MARKING

Simon & Schuster, Inc., licensed by United Media, Brent Edwards, Program Director, MBI 8979/bro

ITEM	SIZE
Advertisement - The Raggedy Ann and Andy Throw Reservation Application	5½ x 8½

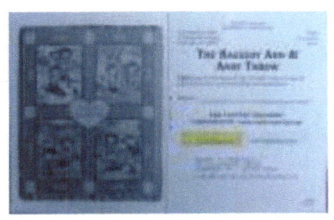

MANUFACTURER/MARKING

MBI 8979/OC

ITEM	SIZE
Advertisement - The Raggedy Ann Rally Sharing the Love Raggedy Style Banquet and Silent Auction place card	3 x 7

MANUFACTURER/MARKING
Yoder's Kitchen, Arthur, IL, Friday, June 7, 2019, 6:00 p.m.

ITEM	SIZE
Advertisement - The Raggedy Ann Rally Sharing the Love Raggedy Style Banquet and Silent Auction place card, James McNamee	3 x 7

MANUFACTURER/MARKING
Yoder's Kitchen, Arthur, IL, Friday, June 7, 2019, 6:00 p.m.

ITEM	SIZE
Advertisement - The Raggedy Ann Rally Sharing the Love Raggedy Style Banquet and Silent Auction place card, Renee Frantzen	3 x 7

MANUFACTURER/MARKING
Yoder's Kitchen, Arthur, IL, Friday, June 7, 2019, 6:00 p.m.

ITEM	SIZE
Advertisement - The Raggedy Family Tree Book Order Form	8½ x 11

MANUFACTURER/MARKING

ITEM | SIZE
Advertisement - The Raggedy School House Grand Opening Celebration! | 8½ x 11

MANUFACTURER/MARKING

Saturday, June 22, 1996, Karen Allen, Spencerport, New York 14559

ITEM | SIZE
Advertisement - The Second Annual Florida Raggedy Ann, Doll and Teddy Bear Convention | 8½ x 11

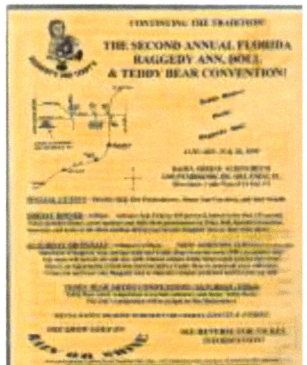

MANUFACTURER/MARKING

January 29 and 30, 1999, Orlando, Florida

ITEM | SIZE
Advertisement - The Snowden, Raggedy Ann and Andy Holiday Show, A Spectacular on Ice | 3¾ x 7

MANUFACTURER/MARKING

CBS Friday, 11/27, 7 p.m. CST, 8 p.m. EST and PST

ITEM | SIZE
Advertisement - The Snowden, Raggedy Ann and Andy Holiday Show, A Spectacular on Ice, half-page | 5⅜ x 8⅝

MANUFACTURER/MARKING

CBS Friday, 11/27, 7 p.m. CST, 8 p.m. EST and PST

ITEM	SIZE
Advertisement - The Snowden, Raggedy Ann and Andy Holiday Show, A Spectacular on Ice, quarter-page, black and white	4⅞ x 7⅜

MANUFACTURER/MARKING

CBS Friday, 11/27, 7 p.m. CST, 8 p.m. EST and PST, Snowden 1998 Dayton Hudson Corp., Raggedy Ann and Andy 1998 Simon & Schuster, Inc.

ITEM	SIZE
Advertisement - Theatre Three Children's Summer Show Performances	6 x 8

MANUFACTURER/MARKING

Raggedy Ann and Andy, July 5-27, Theatre Three 412 Main Street, Port Jefferson, NY 11777

ITEM	SIZE
Advertisement - Theatre Three, Raggedy Ann and Andy Ticket, Seat 103	2 x 5½

MANUFACTURER/MARKING

Theatre Three, 412 Main Street, Port Jefferson, NY 11777, Saturday, July 13, 2024, 11:00 a.m., House Center/Row G/103

ITEM	SIZE
Advertisement - Theatre Three, Raggedy Ann and Andy Ticket, Seat 104	2 x 5½

MANUFACTURER/MARKING

Theatre Three, 412 Main Street, Port Jefferson, NY 11777, Saturday, July 13, 2024, 11:00 a.m., House Center/Row G/104

ITEM	SIZE
Advertisement - There's No Other Angel Like You Certificate of Authenticity	3¼ x 7⅜

MANUFACTURER/MARKING
1999 Simon & Schuster, Inc., Enesco Corp. 597430 93RA531

ITEM	SIZE
Advertisement - There's Nothing Quite as Happy as a Day Full of Sunshine Certificate of Authenticity	3¼ x 7⅜

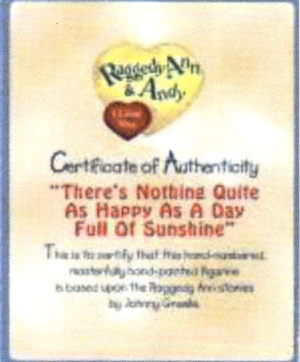

MANUFACTURER/MARKING
Simon & Schuster, Inc., licensed by United Media, Enesco Corp. 045544679817 677787

ITEM	SIZE
Advertisement - Three is a Happy Time for Me Certificate of Authenticity	3¼ x 7⅜

MANUFACTURER/MARKING
Simon & Schuster, Inc., licensed by United Media, Enesco Corp. 045544151955 823724

ITEM	SIZE
Advertisement - Timeless Toys, Girl sitting holding a 30 inch Raggedy Ann	9 x 12

MANUFACTURER/MARKING

ITEM
Advertisement - Tiny Tots Kissy and Huggs Certificate of Authenticity

SIZE
5 x 7

MANUFACTURER/MARKING
2570 Marie Osmond

ITEM
Advertisement - Tiny Tots Rosy and Rags Certificate of Authenticity

SIZE
5 x 7⅞

MANUFACTURER/MARKING
4223 Marie Osmond

ITEM
Advertisement - To have a Friend is to be Happy Certificate of Authenticity

SIZE
3¼ x 7⅜

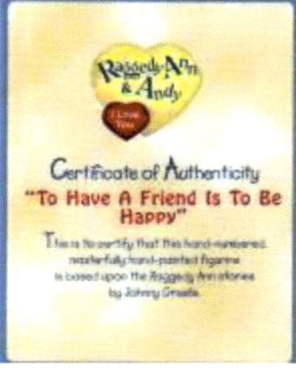

MANUFACTURER/MARKING
Simon & Schuster, Inc., licensed by United Media, Enesco Corp. 045544711876 709050

ITEM
Advertisement - Together We Make a Beat That Makes You Tap Your Feet Certificate of Authenticity

SIZE
3¼ x 7⅛

MANUFACTURER/MARKING
Simon & Schuster, Inc., licensed by United Media, Enesco Corp. 045544471206 864986

ITEM	SIZE
Advertisement - Touch Somebody with a Little Love Today Certificate of Authenticity	3¼ x 7⅜

MANUFACTURER/MARKING

Simon & Schuster, Inc., licensed by United Media, Enesco Corp. 045544711906 709085

ITEM	SIZE
Advertisement - Toys for Tots 1998 Ornament certificate of authenticity	4 x 6

MANUFACTURER/MARKING

ITEM	SIZE
Advertisement - Toys Galore	2⅜ x 4½

MANUFACTURER/MARKING

20" Georgenes

ITEM	SIZE
Advertisement - Treasured Memories	8½ x 11

MANUFACTURER/MARKING

1906 48th Street N.W., Canton, Ohio 44709, 1-800-783-5378 X4438

ITEM	SIZE
Advertisement - Treat for Two Certificate of Authenticity	3¾ x 6¾

MANUFACTURER/MARKING

1999 Simon & Schuster, Inc. A807

ITEM	SIZE
Advertisement - Trick or Treat, You're So Sweet Certificate of Authenticity	3¼ x 7⅜

MANUFACTURER/MARKING

Simon & Schuster, Inc., licensed by United Media, Enesco Corp. 045544272704 104391

ITEM	SIZE
Advertisement - True Friends Certificate of Authenticity	3¼ x 7⅜

MANUFACTURER/MARKING

Simon & Schuster, Inc., Enesco Corp. 045544355025 801267

ITEM	SIZE
Advertisement - T-shirt with rag dolls hanging from a clothesline	5⅜ x 8

MANUFACTURER/MARKING

Endless Designs. Navy/Rag Dolls X0261905

ITEM	SIZE
Advertisement - Turn Four Means So Much More Certificate of Authenticity	3¼ x 7⅜

MANUFACTURER/MARKING	
Simon & Schuster, Inc., licensed by United Media, Enesco Corp. 045544525374 823732	

ITEM	SIZE
Advertisement - Turning Eight Makes You Feel Great Certificate of Authenticity	3¼ x 7⅜

MANUFACTURER/MARKING	
Simon & Schuster, Inc., licensed by United Media, Enesco Corp. 04554466265 823805	

ITEM	SIZE
Advertisement - Turning One is So Much Fun Certificate of Authenticity	3¼ x 7⅜

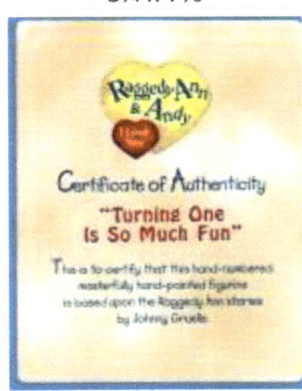

MANUFACTURER/MARKING	
Simon & Schuster, Inc., licensed by United Media, Enesco Corp. 045544525367 823694	

ITEM	SIZE
Advertisement - Turning Seven is a Taste of Heaven Certificate of Authenticity	3¼ x 7⅜

MANUFACTURER/MARKING	
Simon & Schuster, Inc., licensed by United Media, Enesco Corp. 045544372527 823791	

ITEM	SIZE
Advertisement - Two Raggedy Ann and Andy 10K Walks in Arcola, Illinois	5½ x 8½

MANUFACTURER/MARKING

Saturday, June 2, 2012, Raggedy Ann Friendship Gathering, Sunday, June 24, 2012, Walldog Mural Painting

ITEM	SIZE
Advertisement - United of Omaha, Her security is planned…by Electro Analysis	10¼ x 13½

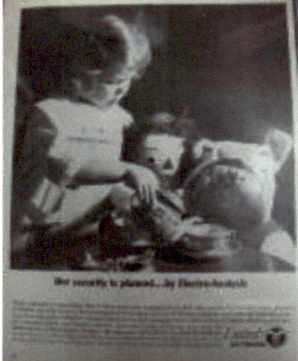

MANUFACTURER/MARKING

Her Security is Planned…by Electro-Analysis

ITEM	SIZE
Advertisement - Upcoming Summer Events at the Stony Brook Village Center	8½ x 11

MANUFACTURER/MARKING

ITEM	SIZE
Advertisement - Vintage Asleep/Awake Dolls Certificate of Authenticity	3¼ x 5⅝

MANUFACTURER/MARKING

2014 Hasbro #0466 of 2400/www.auroraworld.com

ITEM	SIZE
Advertisement - Visit the Johnny Gruelle Raggedy Ann and Andy Museum	3¾ x 8½

MANUFACTURER/MARKING
110 East Main Street, Arcola, Illinois 61910

ITEM	SIZE
Advertisement - Vyverberg's and Johnny Gruelle	8½ x 11

MANUFACTURER/MARKING
Arcola Chamber of Commerce, Johnny Gruelle

ITEM	SIZE
Advertisement - Vyverberg's, Arcola Special Events	8½ x 11

MANUFACTURER/MARKING

ITEM	SIZE
Advertisement - Wanamaker's Jolly Book	8½ x 11

MANUFACTURER/MARKING
Justin Gruelle's Artwork, September 1930

ITEM | SIZE
Advertisement - Wanted: Raggedy Ann Dolls, Books by Johnny Gruelle | 8½ x 11

MANUFACTURER/MARKING

Larry Vaughn

ITEM | SIZE
Advertisement - Welcome to the Raggedy Ann Rally Presenting Johnny's Legacy | 5½ x 8½

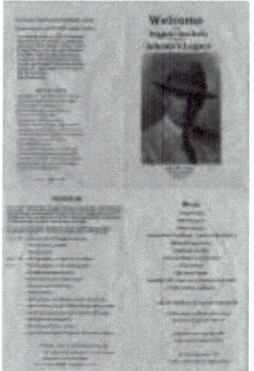

MANUFACTURER/MARKING

June 8 and 9, 2018, Yoder's Kitchen, Arthur, IL

ITEM | SIZE
Advertisement - We'll take any fruit n' cereal as long as it's Post Raisin Bran | 10 x 11¼

MANUFACTURER/MARKING

General Foods, Dick Sargent

ITEM | SIZE
Advertisement - Westbury Music Fair Presents Raggedy Ann and Andy, A Holiday Adventure | 5 x 7

MANUFACTURER/MARKING

Tuesday, December 29

ITEM

Advertisement - What's Old is New, Forever Friends

SIZE

5⅝ x 8¼

MANUFACTURER/MARKING

New Raggedy Ann and Andy set designed by R. John Wright

ITEM

Advertisement - Whenever You're Near Sweet Music I Hear Certificate of Authenticity

SIZE

3¼ x 7⅛

MANUFACTURER/MARKING

Simon & Schuster, Inc., licensed by United Media, Enesco Corp. 0415544471190 864978

ITEM

Advertisement - Wileswood Country Store, 1996 Calendar

SIZE

8½ x 11

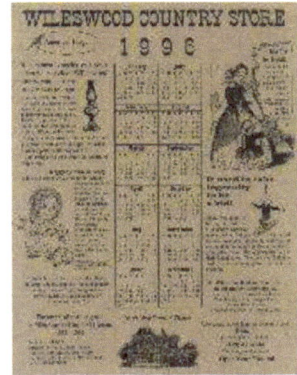

MANUFACTURER/MARKING

ITEM

Advertisement - Wileswood Country Store, Your Door to the Past

SIZE

9 x 16

MANUFACTURER/MARKING

November 1, 1990

ITEM	SIZE
Advertisement - With Love From Mrs. Claus Certificate of Ownership	4½ x 6½

MANUFACTURER/MARKING
1999 Hasbro, Inc., The Danbury Mint A1147, Peter B. Maglathlin, Director

ITEM	SIZE
Advertisement - With Love From Mrs. Claus Posing Instructions	5½ x 8½

MANUFACTURER/MARKING
1999 Hasbro, Inc., SAR/2PC

ITEM	SIZE
Advertisement - With Love From Mrs. Claus Reservation Application	3⅞ x 7¼

MANUFACTURER/MARKING
1998 Hasbro, Inc., SAR of A1147

ITEM	SIZE
Advertisement - Wonderful Raggedy Anns	8½ x 11

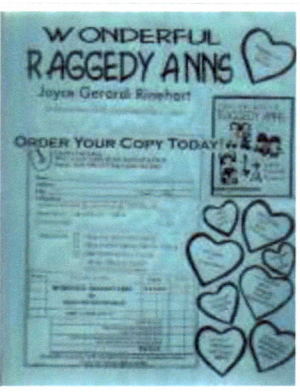

MANUFACTURER/MARKING
A Schiffer Book for Collectors ISBN 0-764302779

ITEM	SIZE
Advertisement - You Get Lots of Kicks When You're Six Certificate of Authenticity	3¼ x 7⅜

MANUFACTURER/MARKING

Simon & Schuster, Inc., licensed by United Media, Enesco Corp. 045544372343 823775

ITEM	SIZE
Advertisement - You Make the World Safe for You and Me Certificate of Authenticity	3¼ x 7⅜

MANUFACTURER/MARKING

Simon & Schuster, Inc., licensed by United Media, Enesco Corp. 045544392747 290947

ITEM	SIZE
Advertisement - Your Friendship is a Special Treat Certificate of Authenticity	3¼ x 7⅜

MANUFACTURER/MARKING

Simon & Schuster, Inc., licensed by United Media, Enesco Corp. 045544272711 104392

ITEM	SIZE
Advertisement - You're a Cut Above the Rest Certificate of Authenticity	3¼ x 7⅜

MANUFACTURER/MARKING

Simon & Schuster, Inc., licensed by United Media, Enesco Corp. 045544389273 288918

ITEM	SIZE
Advertisement - You're Invited to a Valentine's Day Party with Raggedy Ann and Andy	8½ x 11

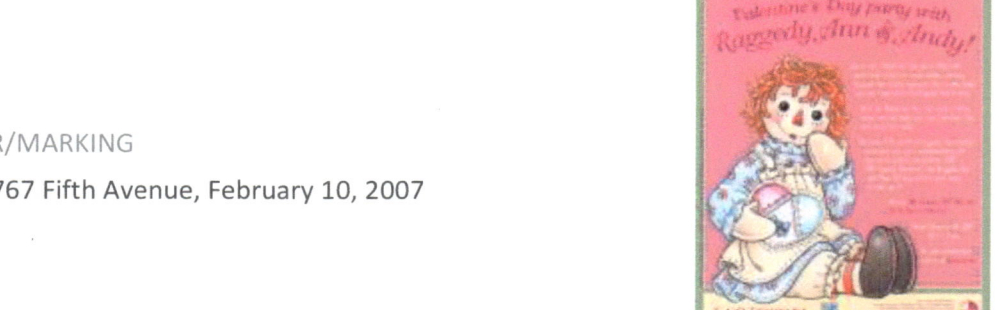

MANUFACTURER/MARKING

F.A.O. Schwarz, 767 Fifth Avenue, February 10, 2007

ITEM	SIZE
Advertisement - Zale's Jewelers	10½ x 13⅝

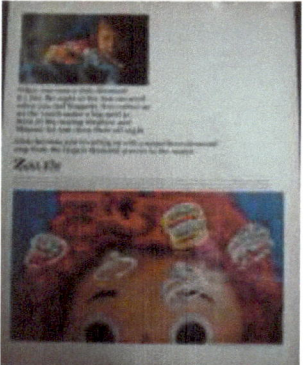

MANUFACTURER/MARKING

1966 Zale Corp.

ITEM	SIZE
Advertisement-Raggedy Ann, Andy and Friends, A unique, month-long doll exhibit for the entire family!	8½ x 11

MANUFACTURER/MARKING

August 1-31, 2007

ITEM	SIZE
Appliance - A Raggedy Ann Story kitchen oven, wood stove, porcelain coated steel and wood, white	10¾ x 11¾ x 14½

MANUFACTURER/MARKING

Simon & Schuster, Inc., licensed by United Media 107/500

ITEM	SIZE
Appliance - Johnny Jump-Up, Country Cousins, baby exerciser for babies up to 24 pounds	8 x 15 x 57

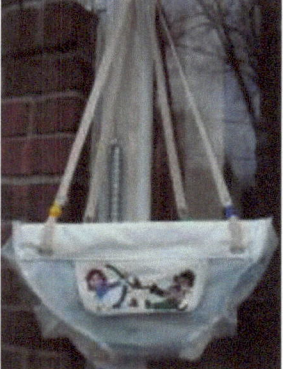

MANUFACTURER/MARKING
An Infanseat Product, Eldora, IA 50627

ITEM	SIZE
Appliance - Raggedy Andy Balloon Blower, black, wood	8 x 19 x 24¼

MANUFACTURER/MARKING

ITEM	SIZE
Appliance - Raggedy Ann and Andy Baby Food Grinder	4⅛ x 4⅛ x 5 15/16

MANUFACTURER/MARKING
1978 The Bobbs-Merrill Co., Inc., Nursery Needs, Sanitoy, Inc. 1706R

ITEM	SIZE
Appliance - Raggedy Ann and Andy Real Push-Button Happy Talk Telephone with stand	3⅝ x 8 x 9

MANUFACTURER/MARKING
1983 The Bobbs-Merrill Co., Inc., Tote, Inc., Oceanport, NJ 07757 #8500

ITEM	SIZE
Appliance - Raggedy Ann ice box, plastic	5½ x 10¾ x 21

MANUFACTURER/MARKING
1978 Hasbro, Inc. M2631

ITEM	SIZE
Appliance - Raggedy Ann sink, plastic	6¼ x 14½ x 20

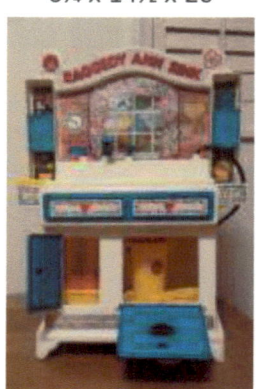

MANUFACTURER/MARKING
1978 Hasbro, Inc. M2578

ITEM	SIZE
Appliance - Raggedy Ann stove, plastic	6¾ x 11½ x 21

MANUFACTURER/MARKING
1978 Hasbro, Inc. M2578

ITEM	SIZE
Appliance - Raggedy Ann's refrigerator, red top and sides, white door, metal	6 x 7½ x 15

MANUFACTURER/MARKING
1970 The Bobbs-Merrill Co., Inc., Gabriel

ITEM	SIZE
Appliance - Raggedy Ann's sink, white top, red sides and front, metal	6½ x 11 x 11¼

MANUFACTURER/MARKING
1970 The Bobbs-Merrill Co., Inc., Gabriel

ITEM	SIZE
Appliance - Raggedy Ann's stove, white top, red sides and front, metal	6½ x 11 x 11¼

MANUFACTURER/MARKING
1970 The Bobbs-Merrill Co., Inc., Gabriel

ITEM	SIZE
Apron - Raggedy Ann and Andy hanging from a kite string, white background, red binding, cross stitch	14½ x 15¼

MANUFACTURER/MARKING

ITEM	SIZE
Apron - Raggedy Ann and Andy wearing blue and red outfits, orange hair, blue and white gingham background, pocket on front	21 x 32¼

MANUFACTURER/MARKING

ITEM	SIZE
Apron - Raggedy Ann and Andy wearing green and yellow outfits, mustard colored vertical stripes on a beige background, quilted has a recipe for Warm Spicy Cider printed on the bodice	23 x 25

MANUFACTURER/MARKING

1976 The Bobbs-Merrill Company, Inc.

ITEM	SIZE
Apron - Raggedy Ann Busy	1½ x 11¾ x 18

MANUFACTURER/MARKING

1969 The Bobbs-Merrill Co., Inc., Made in Japan for Western Publishing Co. 4854

ITEM	SIZE
Apron - Raggedy Ann surrounded by red and blue flowers, white, vinyl	8 x 9½

MANUFACTURER/MARKING

1972 Bobbs-Merrill Co., Inc.

ITEM	SIZE
Apron - Raggedy Ann, Raggedy Andy and Raggedy Arthur on yellow grid lines, ties in the back	Adult Small

MANUFACTURER/MARKING

1980 Bobbs-Merrill Co., Inc.

ITEM	SIZE
Armoire - Raggedy Ann and Andy on doors, blue knobs, white, wood, miniature	1½ x 4¾ x 6¾

MANUFACTURER/MARKING

Binkee, A Division of Pitty Pat Miniatures, Inc.

ITEM	SIZE
Armoire - Two cabinets and a cubby hole, Raggedy Ann and Andy on right side door, white, wood, miniature	1¼ x 3⅛ x 5¼

MANUFACTURER/MARKING

Binkee, A Division of Pitty Pat Miniatures, Inc.

ITEM	SIZE
Article - 10th Annual Raggedy Ann Festival, Cynthiana, Kentucky	8½ x 11

MANUFACTURER/MARKING

ITEM	SIZE
Article - 1930's Raggedy Ann and Andy Pair Sells for $2,000	5¼ x 10½

MANUFACTURER/MARKING

June 20, 1997 issue

ITEM	SIZE
Article - 2011 Arcola Raggedy Friendship Gathering Pull-out Section	23 x 17½

MANUFACTURER/MARKING

ITEM	SIZE
Article - 7th Annual Raggedy Ann and Andy Festival	8½ x 11

MANUFACTURER/MARKING

May 17-19, 1996

ITEM	SIZE
Article - 90th Birthday Raggedy Ann	8½ x 11

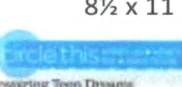

MANUFACTURER/MARKING

ITEM	SIZE
Article - A Child at Heart, by Patricia Hall (10 pages)	8½ x 11

MANUFACTURER/MARKING

The fanciful world of Johnny Gruelle.

ITEM	SIZE
Article - A Country Rag Doll, by Candy Brainard	6 x 7⅜

MANUFACTURER/MARKING

Doll Reader, December 1988-January 1989

ITEM	SIZE
Article - A Doll With a Heart, by Maureen Herrod (6 pages)	8⅜ x 10⅞

MANUFACTURER/MARKING

Born of sorrow, Raggedy Ann's sunny disposition has charmed generations of children.

ITEM	SIZE
Article - A Feast for the Heart - The Raggedy Ann and Andy Festival, by Patricia Hall (2 pages)	8¼ x 10⅞

MANUFACTURER/MARKING

ITEM	SIZE
Article - A Festival of Raggedys, by Marion Sieben-Mahoney (1 page)	8½ x 11

MANUFACTURER/MARKING

For the past four years a sleepy little town in central Illinois has hosted a festival of Raggedy Ann friends.

ITEM

Article - A First-Class Triumph for Doll Collecting, by Burleigh Grimes (2 pages)

SIZE

8½ x 11

MANUFACTURER/MARKING

ITEM

Article - A Gift of Love, Raggedy Ann, photos and Text by William Miller

SIZE

8½ x 11

MANUFACTURER/MARKING

November-December 1990 Vantage

ITEM

Article - A Gruelle Family Tradition: Raggedy Ann and Andy, circa 1992

SIZE

8½ x 11

MANUFACTURER/MARKING

Home of Raggedy Ann and Raggedy Andy, The Last Great Co., 14 Raggedy Lane, Cashiers, NC

ITEM

Article - A Gruelle Family Tradition: Raggedy Ann and Andy, circa 2000

SIZE

8½ x 11

MANUFACTURER/MARKING

Home of Raggedy Ann and Raggedy Andy, The Last Great Co., 14 Raggedy Lane, Cashiers, NC

ITEM

Article - A Mini Photo Tour of (part of) Karen's personal collection at the Raggedy School House

SIZE

8½ x 11

MANUFACTURER/MARKING

Karen Allen's Personal Collection

ITEM

Article - A Piece of Americana - R. John Wright's Raggedy Ann, An Interview with Dolls Magazine Editor Navda Rondon

SIZE

8½ x 11

MANUFACTURER/MARKING

This article also appears in RJW Collector, Volume 9, Summer 2004

ITEM

Article - A Price Guide to Raggedy Ann & Andy by Gertrude Fitzgibbons

SIZE

8½ x 11

MANUFACTURER/MARKING

If you like Raggedy Ann and Andy, you'll find something to pique your interest at the Raggedy Ann Festival in Arcola, IL

ITEM

Article - A Rag Doll That Has Linked Generations, An American Icon, Part I

SIZE

8½ x 11

MANUFACTURER/MARKING

ITEM	SIZE
Article - A Rag Doll That Has Linked Generations, An American Icon, Part II	8½ x 11

MANUFACTURER/MARKING

ITEM	SIZE
Article - A Ragged Tale	4¾ x 5½

MANUFACTURER/MARKING

Raggedy Ann circa 1918

ITEM	SIZE
Article - A Raggedy Empire (1 page), by Lisa Margonelli	8½ x 11

MANUFACTURER/MARKING

The dolls' creator left an inspiring legacy

ITEM	SIZE
Article - A Very Raggedy Assemblage, by William Miller	8½ x 11

MANUFACTURER/MARKING

ITEM	SIZE
Article - Adopt a Family - Christmas 1983	8¼ x 10

MANUFACTURER/MARKING

1974 Bobbs-Merrill Co., Inc.

ITEM	SIZE
Article - All Dressed Up and On With the Show (2 pages)	8½ x 11

MANUFACTURER/MARKING

ITEM	SIZE
Article - And the Winner Is...	5¼ x 8⅞

MANUFACTURER/MARKING

Antique Week, May 13, 2002

ITEM	SIZE
Article - Applause Issues Replicas of Vintage Raggedy Anns	4 x 14

MANUFACTURER/MARKING

Toy Shop, February 27, 1998

ITEM	SIZE
Article - Archives, Hitty, Raggedy Ann, and All the Rest	8½ x 11

MANUFACTURER/MARKING

ITEM	SIZE
Article - Arcola Native Johnny Gruelle: Creator of Raggedy Ann and Andy	3⅞ x 5⅞

MANUFACTURER/MARKING

ITEM	SIZE
Article - Arcola Raggedy Rally	1½ x 3¾

MANUFACTURER/MARKING

ITEM	SIZE
Article - Arcola's Tribute to Johnny Gruelle, Creator of Raggedy Ann	5½ x 8⅝

MANUFACTURER/MARKING

Arcola Chamber of Commerce

ITEM	SIZE
Article - Artist Trading Cards	8½ x 11

MANUFACTURER/MARKING

ITEM	SIZE
Article - Aurora Toy Company Introduces New Raggedys	4 x 9

MANUFACTURER/MARKING

ITEM	SIZE
Article - Behind the Scenes-The Snowden, Raggedy Ann & Andy Holiday Show, by Caitlin Kelly (4 pages)	8½ x 11

MANUFACTURER/MARKING

ITEM	SIZE
Article - Beloved Belindy-Raggedy Ann and Andy's Cheerful Friend, by Candy Brainard (4 pages)	8½ x 11

MANUFACTURER/MARKING

ITEM	SIZE
Article - Beloved Raggedy Ann and Raggedy Andy - A Grandson's Perspective by Kim Gruelle (2 pages)	8½ x 11

MANUFACTURER/MARKING

ITEM	SIZE
Article - Can't Get Enough Raggedy Grins	6¾ x 7⅜

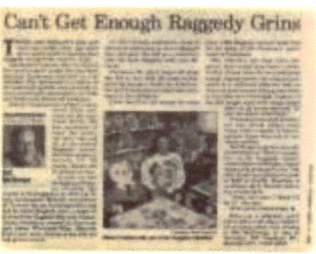

MANUFACTURER/MARKING

My Collection by Bill McTernan

ITEM	SIZE
Article - Carrying on the Family Tradition, by Joni Gruelle (1 page)	8½ x 11

MANUFACTURER/MARKING

ITEM	SIZE
Article - Childhood Love of Raggedy Ann Grows into Big Collection	8½ x 11

MANUFACTURER/MARKING

Suburban News, Issue Number 32, by Barbara Burke

ITEM	SIZE
Article - Collecting Delights: Raggedy Ann & Raggedy Andy by Karen B. Kurtz (4 pages)	8½ x 11

MANUFACTURER/MARKING
Collecting rag dolls has its own unique challenges.

ITEM	SIZE
Article - Collection, A Lifelong Love, by Emily Shapiro	8 1/2 x 11

MANUFACTURER/MARKING
Collection of Paralee Scrivner

ITEM	SIZE
Article - Collector Club 10th Anniversary, by R. John Wright	8½ x 11

MANUFACTURER/MARKING

ITEM	SIZE
Article - Country Getaway, Raggedy Ann Festival in Arcola	8½ x 11

MANUFACTURER/MARKING

ITEM	SIZE
Article - Cover Story-Raggedy Ann & Andy, by Lisa Jacobsen (8 pages)	8½ x 11

MANUFACTURER/MARKING
Johnny Gruelle's storybook creations have captured the hearts of collectors everywhere

ITEM	SIZE
Article - Crafted with Love, Johnny Gruelle's Raggedy Ann and Andy, by Patricia Hall	8½ x 11

MANUFACTURER/MARKING

ITEM	SIZE
Article - Decorating With Your Favorite Things (6 pages)	8½ x 11

MANUFACTURER/MARKING
From Pigs to Pottery, How to Show Off Your Collections

ITEM	SIZE
Article - Doll Club Doings - A Birthday Party for Raggedy Ann as she turns 100, by Helaine Ball Eckstein	8½ x 11

MANUFACTURER/MARKING

ITEM	SIZE
Article - Doll Club Doings - And They Lived Happily Ever After, by Jane Easterly (2 pages)	8½ x 11

MANUFACTURER/MARKING

ITEM	SIZE
Article - Doll Devotion Woman has written 13 books about Raggedy Ann and Andy	4 x 6

MANUFACTURER/MARKING

Carmel Valley, CA, by Kelly O' Connor

ITEM	SIZE
Article - Doll in the Family, The granddaughter of Raggedy Ann's creator makes a monument in Arcola	13⅝ x 22½

MANUFACTURER/MARKING

Lifestyle Herald Review, May 21, 1999

ITEM	SIZE
Article - Dolls and Postcards, by Barry D. Mueller, from the Collection of Renee Frantzen (1 page)	8½ x 11

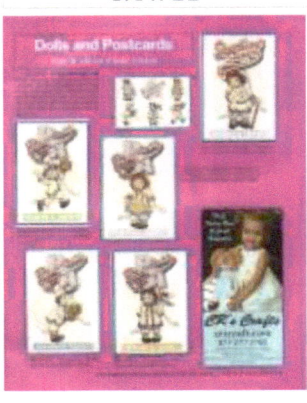

MANUFACTURER/MARKING

ITEM

Article - Dolls and Postcards, by Barry D. Mueller, Postage Stamp Raggedy Ann and Hospital Doll, Paper Doll Greetings (1 page)

SIZE

8½ x 11

MANUFACTURER/MARKING

ITEM

Article - Dolls up for stately honor

SIZE

12⅝ x 22⅞

MANUFACTURER/MARKING

by Kurt Erickson, The Pantagraph, February 21, 2003

ITEM

Article - Dolls with a Heart: The Raggedy Ann Story by Jacqueline Wilson (3 pages)

SIZE

8½ x 11

MANUFACTURER/MARKING

The story behind these comforting, lovable dolls

ITEM

Article - Dorita Alice...just dabbling in my mother's love...the exciting world of dolls by Dorita M. Mortensen

SIZE

8½ x 11

MANUFACTURER/MARKING

Nannie's Shelter for Wayward Raggedies, A rescue and rehab for Raggedies

ITEM	SIZE
Article - Early American Dolls, The Rag Doll, by Doris A. Paul	17 x 11

MANUFACTURER/MARKING

ITEM	SIZE
Article - Everybody Loves a Rag Doll, by Kerra Davis (4 pages)	8½ x 11

MANUFACTURER/MARKING

ITEM	SIZE
Article - Fans for Raggedy Ann	2⅜ x 3⅛

MANUFACTURER/MARKING

The Associated Press

ITEM	SIZE
Article - First Day of Issue Classic American Dolls Raggedy Ann	4¼ x 7½

MANUFACTURER/MARKING

July 28, 1997, Anaheim, CA 92803, Johnny Gruelle's Raggedy Ann

ITEM	SIZE
Article - Friends of Raggedy Ann, by Helaine Ball Eckstein (4 pages)	8½ x 11

MANUFACTURER/MARKING

Carol Hamm, guest speaker

ITEM	SIZE
Article - From Rags to Cyberspace-Trina Chow's Collection, by Lisa Margonelli (1 page)	8½ x 11

MANUFACTURER/MARKING

An artist purts her chidhood passion on the Web.

ITEM	SIZE
Article - Georgene Hopf Averill: The Real Story, by Don Jensen (20 pages)	8½ x 11

MANUFACTURER/MARKING

ITEM	SIZE
Article - Giving Your Ragdolls an Antique Look by Barbara Seeberger	8½ x 11

MANUFACTURER/MARKING

ITEM	SIZE
Article - Gruelle wanted to create books "good for children"	11 x 17⅛

MANUFACTURER/MARKING
Antique Week, July 28, 1997

ITEM	SIZE
Article - Happy Birthday Raggedy Ann and Andy	8½ x 11

MANUFACTURER/MARKING
December 1988 Antiques and Collecting, by Mildred Jailer

ITEM	SIZE
Article - Hello, I'm Raggedy Ann (4 pages)	8½ x 11

MANUFACTURER/MARKING

ITEM	SIZE
Article - Hoosiers at Heart, by J. Kent Calder Managing Editor	8½ x 11

MANUFACTURER/MARKING

ITEM	SIZE
Article - Hospital Visiting Program	8½ x 11

MANUFACTURER/MARKING

ITEM	SIZE
Article - How Candy Hearts for Breakfast Came to Be and Candy Hearts for Breakfast, by Jeannie Sieg	8½ x 11

MANUFACTURER/MARKING

ITEM	SIZE
Article - Huggable Raggedy Ann Doll Turns 75 Today	8½ x 11

MANUFACTURER/MARKING

ITEM	SIZE
Article - I Love Raggedy Ann, by June Attwater	8½ x 11

MANUFACTURER/MARKING

ITEM	SIZE
Article - If Walls Could Talk, As told by Joni Gruelle Wannamaker and Tom Wannamaker (10 pages)	8½ x 11

MANUFACTURER/MARKING

ITEM	SIZE
Article - It's a Real Raggedy Love Affair	11⅞ x 13⅝

MANUFACTURER/MARKING

The Indianapolis Star, Sunday, September 8, 1985

ITEM	SIZE
Article - Jacki Payne Collects Old and Unusual Raggedys	8½ x 11

MANUFACTURER/MARKING

ITEM	SIZE
Article - Johnny Gruelle and Raggedy Ann Time-Line (2 pages)	8½ x 11

MANUFACTURER/MARKING

ITEM	SIZE
Article - Johnny Gruelle, An Artist at Heart, by Acclaimed Raggedy Ann Authority Patricia Hall	8½ x 11

MANUFACTURER/MARKING

ITEM	SIZE
Article - Johnny Gruelle, Creator of Raggedy Ann and Andy	8½ x 11

MANUFACTURER/MARKING

ITEM	SIZE
Article - Johnny Gruelle, Creator of Raggedy Ann and Andy Book Review	8½ x 11

MANUFACTURER/MARKING

ITEM	SIZE
Article - Johnny Mouse and the Woozgoozle	10¼ x 13½

MANUFACTURER/MARKING

ITEM	SIZE
Article - Jumpin' Up Songs, Down - Home Music for Modern Kids	8½ x 11

MANUFACTURER/MARKING

ITEM	SIZE
Article - Largest Rag Doll	5⅞ x 7½

MANUFACTURER/MARKING

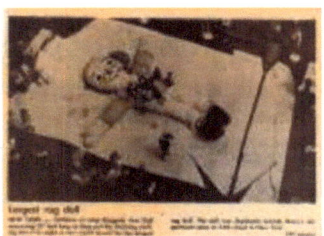

ITEM	SIZE
Article - Leader of the Pack, by Debra Bendis (1 page)	8½ x 11

MANUFACTURER/MARKING

Slip back in time, and once again capture the excitement, the adventures Raggedy Ann brought to your childhood.

ITEM	SIZE
Article - Legendary Dolls	8½ x 11

MANUFACTURER/MARKING

ITEM	SIZE
Article - Local woman's doll collection featured in Raggedy Ann book	14 x 22½

MANUFACTURER/MARKING
Lititz Record Express, Thursday, October 16, 1997

ITEM	SIZE
Article - Lori's Story of Raggedy Ann and Raggedy Andy, by Lori (Boning) Kallweit (2 pages)	8½ x 11

MANUFACTURER/MARKING

ITEM	SIZE
Article - Love and Memories of Raggedy Ann and Andy, What is So Rare as a Day in June, by Lynne Kollmar	8½ x 11

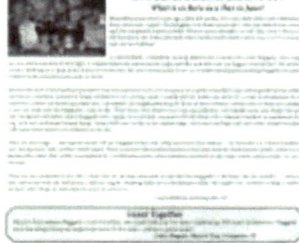

MANUFACTURER/MARKING

ITEM	SIZE
Article - Love in the Dust, by Polly Hacket-Morey © (2 pages)	8½ x 11

MANUFACTURER/MARKING
Collection of Jannell Crosley

ITEM	SIZE
Article - Making Memories, Martha and Kent Melton Bring back the magic of Marcella and Raggedy Ann, by Scott Wood (3 pages)	8 x 10¾

MANUFACTURER/MARKING	
Doll Reader, February 1999	

ITEM	SIZE
Article - Marcella - A Raggedy Ann Story, 2005 Doll & Teddy Bear Expo Show Special	8½ x 11

MANUFACTURER/MARKING

ITEM	SIZE
Article - Marcella and Raggedy Ann by Wendy Lawton	8½ x 11

MANUFACTURER/MARKING

Johnny Gruelle Co., Wendy B. Lawton, Macmillan, Inc.

ITEM	SIZE
Article - Marie Osmond - Doll Enthusiast and Designer, by Sonja Reed (3 pages)	8½ x 11

MANUFACTURER/MARKING

Take a peek at the second career of this multitalented woman.

ITEM	SIZE
Article - Marion Mahoney - Gruelle Dollmaker, by Bill Miller	8½ x 11

MANUFACTURER/MARKING
Talented dollmaker brings Johnny Gruelle's characters to life.

ITEM	SIZE
Article - Marvel at the Comics in Florida	10¾ x 14

MANUFACTURER/MARKING
By E.C.K. Read, March 25, 1997

ITEM	SIZE
Article - Meet the Raggedys	8½ x 11

MANUFACTURER/MARKING

ITEM	SIZE
Article - My Favorite Thing/Raggedy Ann Doll	5½ x 11⅞

MANUFACTURER/MARKING
Mary Davis cherishes the Raggedy Ann doll her mom made for her in 1973

ITEM	SIZE
Article - Nancy Noël: Living the Fantasy Life, by Leslie Alig Collins	8½ x 11

MANUFACTURER/MARKING

ITEM	SIZE
Article - New Rags for Ann	8½ x 11

MANUFACTURER/MARKING

ITEM	SIZE
Article - No Wonder Rag Dolls are the Best Beloved, by Jonathan Green (20 pages)	8½ x 11

MANUFACTURER/MARKING

"As I write this, I have before me on my desk, propped up against the telephone, an old rag doll," wrote Johnny Grulelle, "Dear old Raggedy Ann!"

ITEM	SIZE
Article - Oh, Baby You Don't Look That Old	1¾ x 8¼

MANUFACTURER/MARKING

ITEM

Article - On Loving Dolls, by Dianna Walston

SIZE

8½ x 11

MANUFACTURER/MARKING

ITEM

Article - On Loving Dolls, by Dianna Walston

SIZE

8½ x 11

MANUFACTURER/MARKING

ITEM

Article - Patty Hall, Native Daughter of the Golden West

SIZE

8½ x 11

MANUFACTURER/MARKING

ITEM

Article - Patty Hall's Musical Career

SIZE

8½ x 11

MANUFACTURER/MARKING

Photo by Virginia Curtiss

ITEM	SIZE
Article - Playtime At Alderfer's Antique Doll Auction	10 x 9¼

MANUFACTURER/MARKING

Antiques and The Arts Weekly - September 9, 2005

ITEM	SIZE
Article - Presenting Marcella & Raggedy Ann	8½ x 11

MANUFACTURER/MARKING

ITEM	SIZE
Article - Prudence Brown Gave Us First Raggedy Ann Doll	8½ x 11

MANUFACTURER/MARKING

by Joan Nielsen McHale, The Miami News, July 29, 1962

ITEM	SIZE
Article - R. John Wright - Raggedy Ann (2 pages)	8½ x 11

MANUFACTURER/MARKING

ITEM	SIZE
Article - R. John Wright's Raggedy Ann and Andy Series, by Stephanie Strunk Baker (5 pages)	8½ x 11

MANUFACTURER/MARKING

ITEM	SIZE
Article - Rag Dolls and Love...Too♥, by Beverly Leoczko (3 pages)	8½ x 11

MANUFACTURER/MARKING

From a trash-heap wreck into a doll loaded with charm and sentimental appeal.

ITEM	SIZE
Article - Raggedy Ann - A Spirit of Americana, by Linda White-Francis	8½ x 11

MANUFACTURER/MARKING

ITEM	SIZE
Article - Raggedy Ann - Sweet All the Way Through, by Jan Foulke, Photographs by Howard Foulke (8 pages)	8½ x 11

MANUFACTURER/MARKING

All dolls are from the author's collection unless otherwise noted

ITEM | SIZE
Article - Raggedy Ann Aids Seniors at Complex | 8½ x 11

MANUFACTURER/MARKING

Friday, February 27, 1998 Metro

ITEM | SIZE
Article - Raggedy Ann and Andy "I Love You", Featured at a recent Theriault's Auction | 8½ x 11

MANUFACTURER/MARKING

Photos and information courtesy Theriaults

ITEM | SIZE
Article - Raggedy Ann and Andy Bring Memories of Mother, by Prudence Billings | 6¾ x 7⅜

MANUFACTURER/MARKING

ITEM | SIZE
Article - Raggedy Ann and Andy Collectors, by Kathy Weihe (1 page) | 8½ x 11

MANUFACTURER/MARKING

ITEM	SIZE
Article - Raggedy Ann and Andy Doll Show and Tea Party at the Episcopal Church Home, by Linda Greenfield (2 pages)	8½ x 11

MANUFACTURER/MARKING

ITEM	SIZE
Article - Raggedy Ann and Andy Family Album	5 x 7

MANUFACTURER/MARKING

Schiffer Publishing Co., Ltd.

ITEM	SIZE
Article - Raggedy Ann and Andy Family Album	2⅛ x 6½

MANUFACTURER/MARKING

ISBN: 0-88740-178-3

ITEM	SIZE
Article - Raggedy Ann and Andy Here to Stay	8½ x 11

MANUFACTURER/MARKING

By Andy Wilde

ITEM	SIZE
Article - Raggedy Ann and Andy, by Stephanie Strunk Baker (3 pages)	8½ x 11

MANUFACTURER/MARKING

ITEM	SIZE
Article - Raggedy Ann and Andy, Dolls for All Time by Patricia Hall (8 pages)	8½ x 11

MANUFACTURER/MARKING

ITEM	SIZE
Article - Raggedy Ann and Andy, The Collectibles, by Patricia Hall (3 pages)	8½ x 11

MANUFACTURER/MARKING

ITEM	SIZE
Article - Raggedy Ann and Andy: The Dolls with a Heart, by Kerra Davis	8½ x 11

MANUFACTURER/MARKING

by Kerra Davis, February 2005

ITEM	SIZE
Article - Raggedy Ann and Her Family, reprint of article that appeared in Good Housekeeping 1992	8½ x 11

MANUFACTURER/MARKING
1992 The Hearst Corp., Lutheran Digest by Patricia Caporale

ITEM	SIZE
Article - Raggedy Ann and Raggedy Andy "Made As Only Mollye Can Make Them" (6 pages)	8½ x 11

MANUFACTURER/MARKING
The gifted designs of Mollye Goldman added yet another fascinating chapter to the saga of Raggedy Ann and Andy. Expert Andrew Tabbat tells of the conflict between Gruelle and Goldman, and shares fabulous examples of these delightful dolls.

ITEM	SIZE
Article - Raggedy Ann and Raggedy Andy An Adventure in Time, by Kim Gruelle	8½ x 11

MANUFACTURER/MARKING
All copyrights The Johnny Gruelle Family 1995

ITEM	SIZE
Article - Raggedy Ann and Raggedy Andy, by Bird-Ellen Gage O'Keefe (4 pages)	8½ x 11

MANUFACTURER/MARKING

ITEM	SIZE
Article - Raggedy Ann at 70	8½ x 11

MANUFACTURER/MARKING

ITEM	SIZE
Article - Raggedy Ann Collectibles, Patricia Hall's collection	8½ x 11

MANUFACTURER/MARKING

Ultimate Collector, April 12, 2003

ITEM	SIZE
Article - Raggedy Ann Collection, R. John Wright Dolls (4 pages)	8½ x 11

MANUFACTURER/MARKING

ITEM	SIZE
Article - Raggedy Ann Dress Up Kit	3 x 4⅞

MANUFACTURER/MARKING

Playthings March 1968

ITEM

Article - Raggedy Ann Exhibit-The Many Faces of Raggedy Ann, by Lauren Jaeger (3 pages)

SIZE

8½ x 11

MANUFACTURER/MARKING

A special exhibit at last fall's annual NADDA show captured many hearts.

ITEM

Article - Raggedy Ann Fills Collector's Void

SIZE

8½ x 9¾

MANUFACTURER/MARKING

By Cheryl Sherry

ITEM

Article - Raggedy Ann Finally makes it to National Toy Hall of Fame

SIZE

9½ x 9⅞

MANUFACTURER/MARKING

by Krista Lewin, Journal Gazette and Times Courier, 11/8/2007

ITEM

Article - Raggedy Ann Had Humble Beginnings

SIZE

5¾ x 8½

MANUFACTURER/MARKING

By Anita Richterman

ITEM

Article - Raggedy Ann Honored

SIZE

3 x 5

MANUFACTURER/MARKING

Salem, OR - March 27, 2002 - Toy Hall of Fame

ITEM

Article - Raggedy Ann is Moving

SIZE

5¾ x 6⅜

MANUFACTURER/MARKING

By Patrick Bradley

ITEM

Article - Raggedy Ann Lives On!, by Virginia Davis (4 pages)

SIZE

8½ x 11

MANUFACTURER/MARKING

Helping to keep Raggedy Ann's spirit and popularity alive, several doll artists have chosen to recreate dolls reminiscent of Raggedy Ann and Andy.

ITEM

Article - Raggedy Ann Reigns Supreme for the Holidays, by Helaine Ball Eckstein

SIZE

8½ x 11

MANUFACTURER/MARKING

ITEM	SIZE
Article - Raggedy Ann Slide Program Given at Springfield Library	3 x 3¾

MANUFACTURER/MARKING
Springfield, Illinois Library, Sangamon Valley Doll Study Club

ITEM	SIZE
Article - Raggedy Ann Turns 95 in the Windy City, by UFDC volunteers	8½ x 11

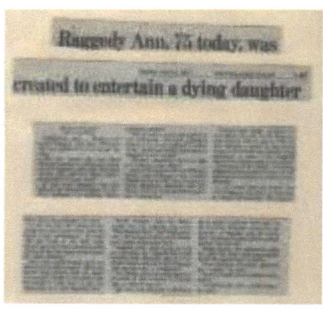

MANUFACTURER/MARKING

ITEM	SIZE
Article - Raggedy Ann, 75 Today, Was Created to Entertain a Dying Daughter, by Denise LaVoie	7 x 7

MANUFACTURER/MARKING
The Philadelphia Inquirer, June 28, 1992

ITEM	SIZE
Article - Raggedy Ann, A Classy Doll, by Sandra Sher	8½ x 11

MANUFACTURER/MARKING
The Post-It is a note from the director of the museum; the magazine was a complimentary copy sent to me several months before my wedding. Underneath is an advertisement for an upcoming exhibit.

ITEM	SIZE
Article - Raggedy Ann, An American Icon	8½ x 11

MANUFACTURER/MARKING

ITEM	SIZE
Article - Raggedy Ann, Andy and Friends	4 x 8

MANUFACTURER/MARKING

ITEM	SIZE
Article - Raggedy Ann, For Eight Decades She's Been America's Favorite Rag Doll, but Don't Tell Andy!	11 x 12

MANUFACTURER/MARKING

ITEM	SIZE
Article - Raggedy Ann, Symbol of Love (3 pages)	8½ x 11

MANUFACTURER/MARKING

ITEM	SIZE
Article - Raggedy Ann, The Traveling Stamp Doll - Alaska, Connecticut, Ohio (4 pages)	8½ x 11

MANUFACTURER/MARKING
http://www.skymicrotec.com/ra

ITEM	SIZE
Article - Raggedy Ann, The Traveling Stamp Doll - California, Hawaii, Illinois	8½ x 11

MANUFACTURER/MARKING
http://www.skymicrotec.com/ra

ITEM	SIZE
Article - Raggedy Ann, The Traveling Stamp Doll - Florida, Kentucky, North Carolina, Virginia	8½ x 11

MANUFACTURER/MARKING
http://www.skymicrotec.com/ra

ITEM	SIZE
Article - Raggedy Ann, The Traveling Stamp Doll - Pennsylvania	8½ x 11

MANUFACTURER/MARKING
http://www.skymicrotec.com/ra

ITEM

Article - Raggedy Ann, The Traveling Stamp Doll- District of Columbia, Georgia, Maryland, New Jersey, South Carolina

SIZE

8½ x 11

MANUFACTURER/MARKING

http://www.skymicrotec.com/ra

ITEM

Article - Raggedy Ann: Over 80 and Still Collectible

SIZE

10½ x 14

MANUFACTURER/MARKING

By Candy Brainard, June 20, 1997

ITEM

Article - Raggedy Ann: The Million Dollar Baby

SIZE

8⅜ x 9⅛

MANUFACTURER/MARKING

by Dee Wedemeyer, The Journal Star, December 24, 1972

ITEM

Article - Raggedy Ann's 100th Birthday Celebration - June 12-13, 2015, Arcola, Illinois (1 page)

SIZE

8½ x 11

MANUFACTURER/MARKING

ITEM	SIZE
Article - Raggedy Ann's 50th Birthday	8½ x 11

MANUFACTURER/MARKING

ITEM	SIZE
Article - Raggedy Books, by Julie Traft (2 pages)	8½ x 11

MANUFACTURER/MARKING
Not just for kids anymore-children's books become collector's items in their own right

ITEM	SIZE
Article - Raggedy Dolls All the Rage	8½ x 11

MANUFACTURER/MARKING
Saturday, April 26, 1997 Homestyle

ITEM	SIZE
Article - Raggedy Facts, by Jerry Kapner	8½ x 11

MANUFACTURER/MARKING
Are you guilty of copyright infringement?

ITEM	SIZE
Article - Raggedy Friendship Gathering in Arcola	8½ x 11

MANUFACTURER/MARKING

ITEM	SIZE
Article - Raggedy Man, Raggedy Ann, by Evelyn Witter (2 pages)	8½ x 11

MANUFACTURER/MARKING

From modest origins Raggedy Ann has grown into a multimillion-dollar industry.

ITEM	SIZE
Article - Raggedy Ruth, Unsuccessful Toys by John West	8½ x 11

MANUFACTURER/MARKING

ITEM	SIZE
Article - Raggedys and Me by Barbara Seeberger (3)	8½ x 11

MANUFACTURER/MARKING

ITEM	SIZE
Article - Raggedys, Raggedys, Raggedys, I am a Raggedy Lover	8½ x 11

MANUFACTURER/MARKING

ITEM	SIZE
Article - Rocking with Raggedy Ann and Andy	8½ x 11

MANUFACTURER/MARKING

Design and Decor - Beth Sherman

ITEM	SIZE
Article - Sand Dollars Doll Club	8½ x 11

MANUFACTURER/MARKING

ITEM	SIZE
Article - Searching for the Real Raggedy, by Patricia Hall (3 pages)	8½ x 11

MANUFACTURER/MARKING

Raggedy Ann has held the attention of children for more than 75 years What magic does she have?

ITEM	SIZE
Article - Sharing...Resources, New Products, Book Reviews, etc. by Kathy Weihe	8½ x 11

MANUFACTURER/MARKING

ITEM	SIZE
Article - She's a Doll of a Lady Who Keeps On Giving	12¼ x 25

MANUFACTURER/MARKING

Senior Scoop, November 29, 2004

ITEM	SIZE
Article - Show and Share by Eva McCarty	8½ x 11

MANUFACTURER/MARKING

Collection of Eva McCarty

ITEM	SIZE
Article - Still Smiling at Seventy-Five, by Patricia L. Hudson	8½ x 11

MANUFACTURER/MARKING

What a doll! For her diamond jubilee, Raggedy Ann and creator Johnny Gruelle have earned a rousing Hoosier salute, Curated by Patricia Hall at Indiana State Museum

ITEM | SIZE
Article - Stuff Kids Buy: It's Raggedy Ann and Andy | 4⅝ x 8

MANUFACTURER/MARKING

by Cassidy Witkowski, Christine Drassos and Rose Marie Dolencie

ITEM | SIZE
Article - Subscribers Share Their Raggedy Dolls | 8½ x 11

MANUFACTURER/MARKING

ITEM | SIZE
Article - Subscribers Sharing Large-Size Play Dolls and Advertising Dolls | 17 x 11

MANUFACTURER/MARKING

ITEM | SIZE
Article - Sunday Ads: Raggedy Indy, Written by Lisa Lorentz on March 8, 2015 | 8½ x 11

MANUFACTURER/MARKING

Written by Lisa Lorentz on March 8, 2015

ITEM	SIZE
Article - Taking His Case to the People	6¼ x 10⅛

MANUFACTURER/MARKING

Daily News August 24, 2005

ITEM	SIZE
Article - The 3rd Raggedy Friendship Gathering 2011	8½ x 11

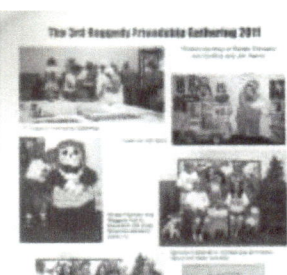

MANUFACTURER/MARKING

Photos courtesy of Renee Frantzen and Cynthia and Jim Heims

ITEM	SIZE
Article - The Adventures of Raggedy Ann and Andy, An Investment in Americana	8½ x 11

MANUFACTURER/MARKING

ITEM	SIZE
Article - The Adventures of Raggedy Ann and Raggedy Andy by Johnny Gruelle	4¼ x 8¾

MANUFACTURER/MARKING

Raggedy Ann and Raggedy Andy and Little Ned Gnome were enjoying the sodas

ITEM

Article - The Adventures of Raggedy Ann and Raggedy Andy by Johnny Gruelle

SIZE

4¼ x 9⅝

MANUFACTURER/MARKING

It wasn't a bit nice for the mean little old witch

ITEM

Article - The Adventures of Raggedy Ann and Raggedy Andy by Johnny Gruelle

SIZE

4¼ x 9¼

MANUFACTURER/MARKING

Wanda Witch was very angry at Raggedy Ann and Andy

ITEM

Article - The Adventures of Raggedy Ann and Raggedy Andy by Johnny Gruelle

SIZE

4¼ x 8¾

MANUFACTURER/MARKING

When the Raggedys and Little Ned Gnome reached the

ITEM

Article - The Adventures of Raggedy Ann and Raggedy Andy by Johnny Gruelle

SIZE

4¼ x 8¾

MANUFACTURER/MARKING

The two mean little old witches had made up

ITEM	SIZE
Article - The Adventures of Raggedy Ann and Raggedy Andy by Johnny Gruelle	4¼ x 13¾

MANUFACTURER/MARKING

That was a dandy fine party Raggedy Ann and Raggedy Andy

ITEM	SIZE
Article - The Adventures of Raggedy Ann and Raggedy Andy by Johnny Gruelle	4¼ x 12½

MANUFACTURER/MARKING

Did you notice how peevish the two mean little

ITEM	SIZE
Article - The Adventures of Raggedy Ann and Raggedy Andy by Johnny Gruelle	4¼ x 11¾

MANUFACTURER/MARKING

I guess I will just keep little old Winda Witch's

ITEM	SIZE
Article - The Adventures of Raggedy Ann and Raggedy Andy by Johnny Gruelle	4¼ x 11¼

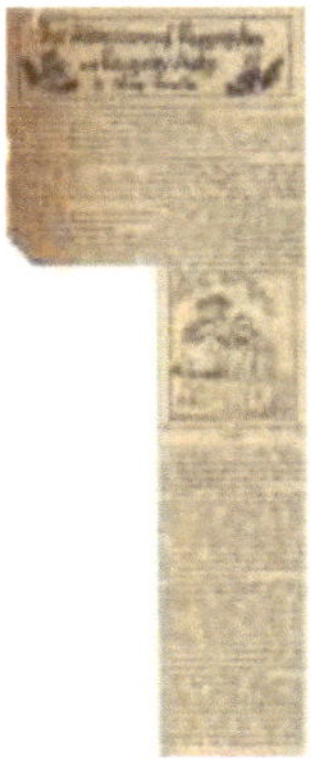

MANUFACTURER/MARKING

It is funny the two mean little old witches

ITEM	SIZE
Article - The Adventures of Raggedy Ann and Raggedy Andy by Johnny Gruelle	4¼ x 8¾

MANUFACTURER/MARKING	
The candy covered cookies are better than raw	

ITEM	SIZE
Article - The Adventures of Raggedy Ann and Raggedy Andy by Johnny Gruelle	4¼ x 9⅛

MANUFACTURER/MARKING	
Well Raggedy Andy cried as he ran up to the top of	

ITEM	SIZE
Article - The Adventures of Raggedy Ann and Raggedy Andy by Johnny Gruelle	4¼ x 15¼

MANUFACTURER/MARKING	
In the deep, deep woods filled with fairies	

ITEM	SIZE
Article - The Adventures of Raggedy Ann and Raggedy Andy by Johnny Gruelle	4¼ x 10⅛

MANUFACTURER/MARKING	
The two mean little old witches looked funny	

ITEM	SIZE
Article - The Adventures of Raggedy Ann and Raggedy Andy by Johnny Gruelle	4¼ x 10⅛

MANUFACTURER/MARKING

Raggedy Ann and Raggedy Andy were glad they had found the ice cream

ITEM	SIZE
Article - The Adventures of Raggedy Ann and Raggedy Andy by Johnny Gruelle	4¼ x 10⅛

MANUFACTURER/MARKING

Raggedy Ann and Raggedy Andy and Little Ned Gnome went singing through

ITEM	SIZE
Article - The Adventures of Raggedy Ann and Raggedy Andy by Johnny Gruelle	4¼ x 8

MANUFACTURER/MARKING

Grampy Groundhog was very thankful...

ITEM	SIZE
Article - The Adventures of Raggedy Ann and Raggedy Andy by Johnny Gruelle	4¼ x 7⅞

MANUFACTURER/MARKING

What do you think Raggedy Ann and Raggedy Andy?

ITEM	SIZE
Article - The Adventures of Raggedy Ann and Raggedy Andy by Johnny Gruelle	4¼ x 7¾

MANUFACTURER/MARKING

Wallie and Winnie Woodpecker could not drink

ITEM	SIZE
Article - The Adventures of Raggedy Ann and Raggedy Andy by Johnny Gruelle	4¼ x 7¾

MANUFACTURER/MARKING

Raggedy Ann and Raggedy Andy and Little Ned Gnome after they had

ITEM	SIZE
Article - The Adventures of Raggedy Ann and Raggedy Andy by Johnny Gruelle	4¼ x 7⅝

MANUFACTURER/MARKING

The Raggedys and Little Ned Gnome found a lot of hot

ITEM	SIZE
Article - The Adventures of Raggedy Ann and Raggedy Andy by Johnny Gruelle	4¼ x 7⅝

MANUFACTURER/MARKING

It isn't much fun being captured by two mean

ITEM	SIZE
Article - The Adventures of Raggedy Ann and Raggedy Andy by Johnny Gruelle	4¼ x 7½

MANUFACTURER/MARKING
Raggedy Andy fooled the two little old sister witches

ITEM	SIZE
Article - The Adventures of Raggedy Ann and Raggedy Andy by Johnny Gruelle	4¼ x 6⅝

MANUFACTURER/MARKING
It was lucky for Little Ned Gnome that

ITEM	SIZE
Article - The Adventures of Raggedy Ann and Raggedy Andy by Johnny Gruelle	4¼ x 10½

MANUFACTURER/MARKING
I'm glad the mean little old witch's magical

ITEM	SIZE
Article - The Adventures of Raggedy Ann and Raggedy Andy by Johnny Gruelle	4¼ x 8¾

MANUFACTURER/MARKING
Raggedy Ann was right when she said the two mean

ITEM	SIZE
Article - The Adventures of Raggedy Ann and Raggedy Andy by Johnny Gruelle	4¼ x 9⅜

MANUFACTURER/MARKING

Wanda and Winda Witch were very angry at the Raggedys

ITEM	SIZE
Article - The Adventures of Raggedy Ann and Raggedy Andy by Johnny Gruelle, Dear Me, Here Comes Mr. Doodle	4¼ x 8¼

MANUFACTURER/MARKING

The Globe, Toronto, Saturday, December 30, 1922

ITEM	SIZE
Article - The Adventures of Raggedy Ann and Raggedy Andy by Johnny Gruelle, The Pirate Captain	8½ x 8⅝

MANUFACTURER/MARKING

The Globe, Toronto, Saturday, June 30, 1923

ITEM	SIZE
Article - The Cruise of the Rickety-Robin	10¼ x 13½

MANUFACTURER/MARKING

November 1921 Woman's World

ITEM	SIZE
Article - The Dolls in Your Life, Case Study Number One: Ginger Snips, by Susanna Oroyan	8 x 10¾

MANUFACTURER/MARKING

ITEM	SIZE
Article - The Dwarfies, by Johnny Gruelle	8⅜ x 11⅝

MANUFACTURER/MARKING

January 1921 Good Housekeeping by Johnny Gruelle

ITEM	SIZE
Article - The Golden Penny, A Johnny Mouse and the Woozgoozle Story	10¼ x 13½

MANUFACTURER/MARKING

July-August 1921 Woman's World

ITEM	SIZE
Article - The Irresistible Quacky Doodles Family, by Patricia Hall (5 pages)	8½ x 11

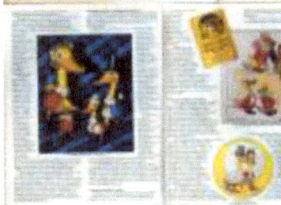

MANUFACTURER/MARKING

ITEM	SIZE
Article - The Life and Times of Raggedy Ann and Andy, by Kerra Davis (3 pages)	8½ x 11

MANUFACTURER/MARKING

ITEM	SIZE
Article - The Magic Pancakes, A Johnny Mouse and the Woozgoozle Story	10¼ x 13½

MANUFACTURER/MARKING

ITEM	SIZE
Article - The Magical Hour, When the Dolls Come to Life, UFDC Special Event (2 pages)	8½ x 11

MANUFACTURER/MARKING

ITEM	SIZE
Article - The Many Faces of Volland-Raggedy Ann and Friends, by Barbara Lauver (6 pages)	8½ x 11

MANUFACTURER/MARKING

ITEM	SIZE
Article - The Market Value of Animation Art	8½ x 11

MANUFACTURER/MARKING

ITEM	SIZE
Article - The Original Raggedy Ann was a Brunette	7⅝ x 10⅞

MANUFACTURER/MARKING

by Kim Gruelle, Reminisce Extra, August 1994

ITEM	SIZE
Article - The Raggedy Ann Festival, Where a Collector Can Find Everything, by Bill Miller	8½ x 11

MANUFACTURER/MARKING

This article is more than one page. The magazine it came from was purchased second hand and several pages are missing.

ITEM	SIZE
Article - The Raggedy Ann Man	8½ x 11

MANUFACTURER/MARKING

Arcola, Illinois, birthplace of Johnny Gruelle

ITEM	SIZE
Article - The Raggedy Ann Man, The Indianapolis Influences of Raggedy Ann Creator Johnny Gruelle (3 pages)	8½ x 11

MANUFACTURER/MARKING

ITEM	SIZE
Article - The Raggedy Story, by Lisa Margonelli (2 pages)	8½ x 11

MANUFACTURER/MARKING

ITEM	SIZE
Article - The Raindrop Soldiers, by Johnny Gruelle	8½ x 11

MANUFACTURER/MARKING

Woman's World for June 1928

ITEM	SIZE
Article - The Real Story of Raggedy Ann, by Robert Reed (2 pages)	8½ x 11

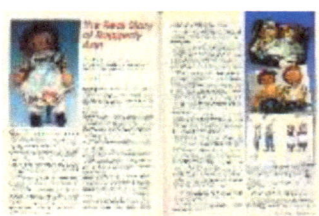

MANUFACTURER/MARKING

How often does a legend spring from an actual event? It's difficult to trace much of folklore. However, this American fairy tale is truly based in reality.

ITEM	SIZE
Article - The Story of a Father's Love - Raggedy Ann and Andy, by Carole Shelley Yates (5 pages)	8½ x 11

MANUFACTURER/MARKING

ITEM	SIZE
Article - The Toy That Says I Love You	6 x 8½

MANUFACTURER/MARKING

Kathy Gleason's Collection

ITEM	SIZE
Article - The True Story of Marcella and Raggedy Ann by Andrew Tabbat (1 page)	8½ x 11

MANUFACTURER/MARKING

ITEM	SIZE
Article - Theatre Three's Raggedy Ann and Andy will become your new buddies, pals and friends	8½ x 10

MANUFACTURER/MARKING

ITEM	SIZE
Article - Theriault's Annual January Doll and Toy Auction in Newport Beach Reaches $2,000,000	8½ x 11

MANUFACTURER/MARKING

ITEM	SIZE
Article - These Dolls Were Small in Size, but Long On Charm	10½ x 14

MANUFACTURER/MARKING
By Kerra Davis, June 20, 1997

ITEM	SIZE
Article - Toyfest '97: A Raggedy Adventure	8½ x 11

MANUFACTURER/MARKING
August 23-25, 1997

ITEM	SIZE
Article - Uncle Clem, Raggedy Ann's Collectible Relative	8½ x 11

MANUFACTURER/MARKING
by Andrew Tabbat

ITEM	SIZE
Article - Uncle Johnny Gruelle's Page for Good Boys and Girls	10¼ x 13½

MANUFACTURER/MARKING

February 1919 Woman's World

ITEM	SIZE
Article - Weeble-Minded and Proud of It!	11 x 14

MANUFACTURER/MARKING

by Mary David

ITEM	SIZE
Article - Welcome to the Doll House, Boulder Crafter Measures Her Life in Dolls	11⅞ x 14¼

MANUFACTURER/MARKING

Lisa Marshall, Daily Camera, Thursday, April 7, 2005

ITEM	SIZE
Article - Wendy Lawton's Marcella and Raggedy Ann, by John Axe	7½ x 9¾

MANUFACTURER/MARKING

Doll Reader, December 1988-January 1989 by John Axe

ITEM	SIZE
Article - When Porcelain Meets Fiction, by Louise Fecher, Photos by Lynton Gardiner	8½ x 11

MANUFACTURER/MARKING

Inspired by children's books and poetry, California artist Wendy Lawton has, in a decade of dollmaking, brought to life many favorite characters.

ITEM	SIZE
Article - Wonderful Raggedy Anns	3⅞ x 5⅜

MANUFACTURER/MARKING

Joyce Gerardi Rinehart, A Schiffer Book for Collectors

ITEM	SIZE
Audio Tape - Raggedy Ann Learns a Lesson and Raggedy Ann and Raggedy Andy	2⅝ x 4¼

MANUFACTURER/MARKING

1978 The Bobbs-Merrill Co., Inc., Society for Visual Education, Inc.

ITEM	SIZE
Audio Tape - Raggedy Andy's Smile	2⅝ x 4¼

MANUFACTURER/MARKING

1978 The Bobbs-Merrill Co., Inc., Society for Visual Education, Inc.

ITEM	SIZE
Audio Tape - Raggedy Ann & Andy Bend and Stretch	2⅝ x 4¼

MANUFACTURER/MARKING
1976, 1978, 1980 The Bobbs-Merrill Co., Inc., Columbia House, CBS, Inc., Kid Stuff KST4012

ITEM	SIZE
Audio Tape - Raggedy Ann and Andy Talking Story Book, Find Somebody Who Needs Ya, Read and Sing Along	7½ x 12½

MANUFACTURER/MARKING

ITEM	SIZE
Audio Tape - Raggedy Ann and Andy Telling Time is Fun	2½ x 4

MANUFACTURER/MARKING
1982 The Bobbs-Merrill Co., Inc., T.J.E. Distributing KST4017

ITEM	SIZE
Audio Tape - Raggedy Ann and Andy, A Musical Adventure, 8-track	⅞ x 4 x 5¼

MANUFACTURER/MARKING
1977 CBS, Inc., Columbia House TC8SA34686

ITEM	SIZE
Audio Tape - Raggedy Ann Stories	4½ x 6

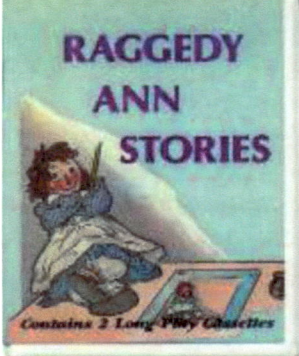

MANUFACTURER/MARKING

1982 Cassette Book Co., Bobbs-Merrill Co., Inc. 850